Lon Chaney's
Dracula - 1930

Books by
Philip J Riley

## CLASSIC HORROR FILMS
*Frankenstein, the original 1931 shooting script*
*Bride of Frankenstein, the original 1935 shooting script*
*Son of Frankenstein, the original 1939 shooting script*
*Ghost of Frankenstein, the original 1942 shooting script*
*Frankenstein Meets the Wolfman, the original 1943 shooting script*
*House of Frankenstein, the original 1944 shooting script*
*The Mummy, the original 1932 shooting script*
*The Mummy's Curse the original 1944 shooting script (as Editor in Chief)*
*The Wolfman, the original 1941 shooting script*
*Dracula, the original 1931 shooting script*
*House of Dracula, the original 1945 shooting script*

## CLASSIC COMEDY FILMS
*Abbott & Costello Meet Frankenstein, the original 1948 shooting script*

## CLASSIC SCIENCE FICTION
*This Island Earth, the original 1955 shooting script*
*The Creature from the Black Lagoon, the original 1953 shooting script (editor-in-chief)*

## THE ACKERMAN ARCHIVES SERIES - LOST FILMS
*The Reconstruction of London After Midnight, the original 1927 shooting script*
*The Reconstruction of A Blind Bargain, the original 1922 shooting script*
*The Reconstruction of The Hunchback of Notre Dame, the original 1923 shooting script*

## CLASSIC SILENT FILMS
*The Reconstruction of The Phantom of the Opera, the original 1925 shooting script*

## FILMONSTER SERIES - LOST SCRIPTS
James Whale's Dracula's Daughter, 1934
Cagliostro, The King of the Dead, 1932
Wolfman vs Dracula 1944
Lon Chaney's Dracula - 1930

## AS EDITOR
*Countess Dracula by Carroll Borland*
*My Hollywood, when both of us were young by Patsy Ruth Miller*
*Mr. Technicolor - Herbert Kalmus*
*Famous Monster of Filmland #2 by Forrest J Ackerman*

## FILM DOCUMENTARIES
A Thousand Faces - as contributor (Photoplay Productions)
Universal Horrors - as contributor (Photoplay Productions)

Mr. Riley has also contributed to 12 film related books by various authors
as well as numerous magazine articles and received the Count Dracula Society Award
and was inducted into Universal's Horror Hall of Fame

# DRACULA
## Starring
## Lon Chaney

An Alternate History for Classic Film Monsters

by

Philip J. Riley

Hollywood Publishing Archives

Published by:
BearManor Media
P O Box 71426
Albany, GA 31708
Phone: 760-709-9696
Fax: 814-690-1559
books@benohmart.com

©2010 Philip J Riley
For Copyright purposes
Philip J Riley is the author in the form of this book

Lon Chaney name and likeness are trademarks of Chaney Enterprises
Treatment of Dracula by Louis Bromfield July 1930
Incomplete script by Louis Bromfield and Dudley Murphy August 1930
Script for Nosferatu by Henrik Galeen (annotation by F. W. Murnau in bold print).
First published in "Murnau" by Lotte Eisner

Cover Art - ©2010 By Philip J Riley - Since none of the scripts in this series were thought to exist and were never produced, we have created mock-up posters in the vintage style of the period.

All photographs are from the Author's collection unless noted

The Author would like to thank the following individuals who contributed and helped make this series possible. Carl Laemmle Jr., R.C.Sherriff, Stanley Bergerman, Gloria Holden, Jane Wyatt, Otto Kruger, Marcel Delgado, Robert Florey, Paul Ivano (Cinematographer), Paul Malvern (producer), Elsa Lanchester, Merion C Cooper, Patric Leroux, Bette Davis, Bela G.. Lugosi, Sara Karloff, Technicolor Corporation, John Balderston II, Douglas Norwine, Loeb and Loeb Attorneys, David Stanley Horsley, Bernard Schubert, John Teehan

Author's Note: I interviewed the producers, directors, stars, cast and crew in the early to late 1970s. They were recalling events that happened 35-45 years previous and sometimes memory fades or events are recalled from their perspective point of view.

First Edition
10 9 8 7 6 5 4 3 2 1

The purpose of this series is the preservation of the art of writing for the screen. Rare books have long been a source of enjoyment and an investment for the serious collector, and even in limited editions there are thousands printed. Scripts, however, numbered only 50 at the most. In the history of American Literature, the screenwriter was being lost in time. It is my hope that my efforts bring about a renewed history and preservation of a great American Literary form, The Screenplay, by preserving them for study by future generations.
Recommended reading -For more information on Lon Chaney or Dracula
"Hollywood Gothic" and "The Monster Show" by David J Skal
" The Lon Chaney trilogy" by Michael F. Blake

**This volume is Dedicated to:**

Carl Laemmle Jr.

*Carl Laemmle Sr. and Carl Laemmle Jr. circa 1936*

*A composite shot of Chaney as "The man in the Beaver Hat"
from London After Midnight, MGM 1927 and a publicity shot of
Bela Lugosi from the opening scene*

*One of two frames of the Newcombe shots which are all that remains today of MGM's 1927 London After Midnight a thinly veiled version of Dracula starring Lon Chaney and directed by Tod Browning*

1929, The Stock Market Crash, at MGM Studios, Lon Chaney's champion Irving Thalberg was in the middle of a power struggle. Tod Browning had moved to Universal Studios and Carl Laemmle Jr. wanted to make a film version of the book "Dracula" by Bram Stoker, an Englishman who has died in 1912 leaving the rights to his works to his wife Florence.

As noted by film historian David J. Skal Chaney and Browning had talked about making the same film as early as 1922.

The Browning-Chaney team together produce the most macabre motion pictures of the 1920s. But none of their collective productions were ever considered a monster film like Dracula or Frankenstein.

When Carl Laemmle Jr. was given control of Universal Pictures he was given permission to do a film version of Dracula and he wanted Lon Chaney to star. And he was told by his father that the only way he could make the picture is by securing Chaney as the lead or possible in a duel role of Count Dracula and Professor Van Helsing.

" I saw the play version of "Dracula" when I went on a trip to New York City and knew that it would make a great film. I had stayed in touch, casually, with Lon Chaney after he left Universal Pictures for Metro-Goldwyn-Mayer. But I had no real power at the studio and when I approached my father he was in the middle of trying to get him to do a sound remake of *The Phantom of the Opera* (1925). He told me the only way he would allow a production of Dracula was if I could get Chaney to star in the picture. He [Laemmle Sr.] knew of the legal entanglements Murnau's company had with Bram Stoker's widow, (eventually we bought a print and script of Dracula which Prana had called Nosferatu) and I knew there was some reluctance by MGM to film Chaney's London After Midnight in 1927. (The same year as John Balderston's play opened in New York City. I don't remember if I saw Bela Lugosi in the lead role, but I knew I had to produce a film version, despite what Prana and Thalberg had to go through."

[Florence Stoker, Bram Stoker's widow had sued the German production company for not securing the rights to film Dracula and won. The court ordered all prints destroyed, but fortunately this was not completely successful.]

Despite all the inner-office opposition, Laemmle Jr. tried to get a three picture deal out of Lon Chaney.

*Eleanor Holm, Howard Hughes, now a studio owner himself at a banquet with Sandra Shaw and Carl Laemmle Jr*

Chaney had already said no to a sound remake of The Phantom and had yet to make his talking debut at this time. But it still didn't stop Laemmle Jr. and a contract was drawn up with this letter, provided to me by the Earnest Goodman, head of copyrights for Universal's Legal Department in 1989 which he called ancient documents from the law firm of Lobe and Lobe:
[attachment- single page]

It is unknown if Mr. Chaney will play a duel role: Count Dracula and Van Helsing.

The letter:
*"June 23, 1929*

*We are enclosing herewith three copies of the proposed agreement with Lon Chaney. Will you be good enough to give special attention to the examination of this contract in order to ascertain whether or not it fully complies with the understanding between yourselves and Mr Chaney.*
*You will, of course, notice that the within contract is somewhat larger than the contract which Chaney had for The Phantom of the Opera, but in view of the fact that some difficulties were encountered in the production of that picture, we have deemed it advisable to include in the within contract all possible precautions.*
*While we do not know whether or not you desire to carry insurance on Chaney during this period of production we have included a clause allowing you to do so, and requiring Chaney to submit to the usual examination for that purpose. Mr. Stern did not specfy if Chaney has, in fact, agreed to a dual role."*

The letter contains an annotation:

"Jr. Emphatic -- keep Stern away from Chaney"
{Walter Stern was Universal's business manager at the time]

In July of 1929 Universal's lawyer Sigfreid Hartman sent a telegram to Edwin Loeb:

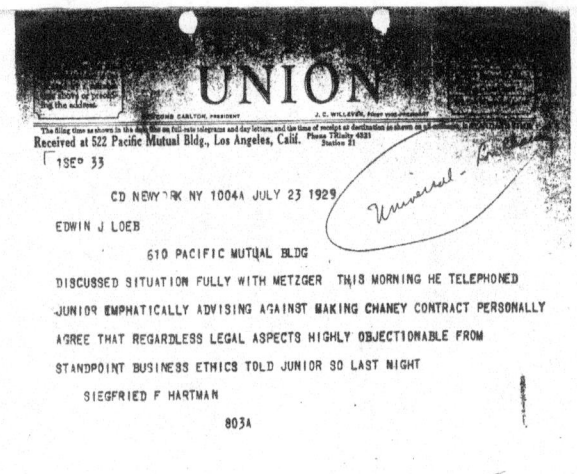

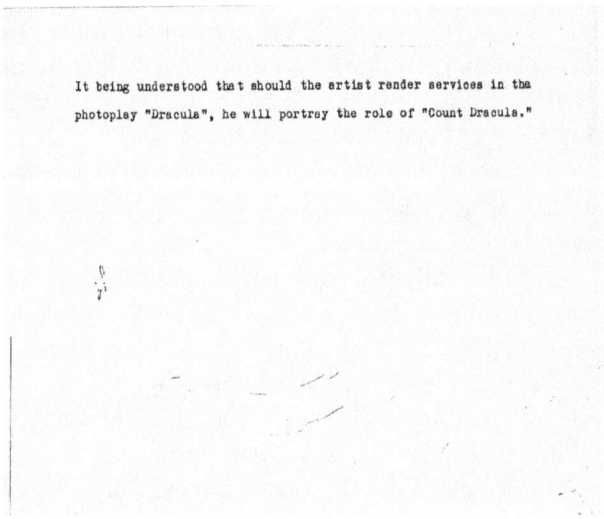

*An additional attachment to the Loeb and Loeb proposed Dracula Contract for Lon Chaney*

Universal City, California,
July ____, 1929.

Mr. Lon Chaney,
c/o Universal Pictures Corporation,
Universal City, California.

Dear Mr. Chaney:

You have heretofore rendered your services for us in connection with our photoplay entitled "Phantom of the Opera", which photoplay has heretofore been released and distributed as a silent picture. We are at present contemplating, producing, releasing, distributing and/or exhibiting a "synchronized", "sound", and/or "talking" version or versions of said photoplay, and we desire to substitute a "double" in your place for use in connection with reproductions of your voice and of certain of your acts, poses, plays and appearances in connection with said photoplay, and you are willing to grant us the right to substitute a "double" in your place. This will accordingly confirm the following agreement between us:

1. You hereby give, grant, transfer, sell and assign to us the right to substitute a "double" in your place for use in connection with reproductions of your voice and as well for all instrumental, musical and other sound effects produced and/or purported to be produced by you in connection with your acts, poses, plays and appearances in our photoplay entitled "Phantom of the Opera", it being expressly agreed that recordations and/or reproductions of the voice of the "double" who is substituted for you may be made and/or used either in English or in any other language or languages.

2. You further give, grant, transfer, sell and assign to us the right to substitute a "double" in your place for use in connection with photographs and/or reproductions of all or any of your acts, poses, plays and appearances, in connection with said photoplay, excepting only so-called "close-ups" of your face, it being understood that we shall not substitute a "double" for you in connection with the reproduction of "close-ups" of your face.

3. We shall have the right, subject, of course, to the provisions of the contract under the terms of which you rendered your services for us in the production of said photoplay to advertise, exploit and/or publicize the "synchronized", "sound", and/or "talking" version or versions of said photoplay to be produced by us in any manner or form which we may desire, subject only to the following conditions and agreements:

(a) We agree that we will not on the screen or in advertising, exploitation and/or publicity issued by us or directly under our control, connect with your name a statement of the fact that you either do or that you do not talk in said photoplay, it being intended by the foregoing portion of this subdivision (a) that any statement on the screen or in advertising, exploitation and/or publicity issued as aforesaid to the effect that any member of the cast of said photoplay either does or does not talk in said photoplay, shall not be connected with or refer to the name "Lon Chaney". It is expressly agreed that the foregoing limitation shall apply only to the name "Lon Chaney" and not to the character portrayed by you in said photoplay. For example, we shall have the right to advertise "The Phantom Talks" or to advertise said character in any other manner we may desire, provided that your name is not used in a statement that said character either does or does not talk.

4. You expressly agree that you will at all times maintain and preserve the utmost secrecy with reference to the fact that a "double" has been used either for reproductions of your voice or of your acts, poses, plays and appearances, or of any instrumental, musical, or other sound effects produced by you, and you agree that you will not at any time disclose or mention to any person, firm or corporation, either orally or in writing, that such "double" has been used. It is expressly agreed that you shall not be called upon to render your personal services or to devote any time to the production of the "synchronized", "sound" and/or "talking" version or versions of said photoplay. It is, of course, understood that we shall own, and you hereby give and grant to us all rights of every kind and character in and to all recordations and/or reproductions made as aforesaid, and shall have the sole and exclusive right to sell, lease, license and generally deal and traffic in the "synchronized", "sound", and/or "talking" version or versions of said photoplay to be produced by us as aforesaid.

In consideration of your execution of this agreement and of your consent and agreement to all of the terms, conditions and provisions hereof, we have paid you concurrently with the execution hereof the sum of Twenty-five Thousand Dollars ($25,000.00), receipt whereof is hereby acknowledged.

If the foregoing is in accordance with your understanding of our agreement, kindly indicate your approval and acceptance thereof in the space hereinbelow provided.

Very truly yours,

UNIVERSAL PICTURES CORPORATION,

By_____

APPROVED AND ACCEPTED:

_____
(Lon Chaney)

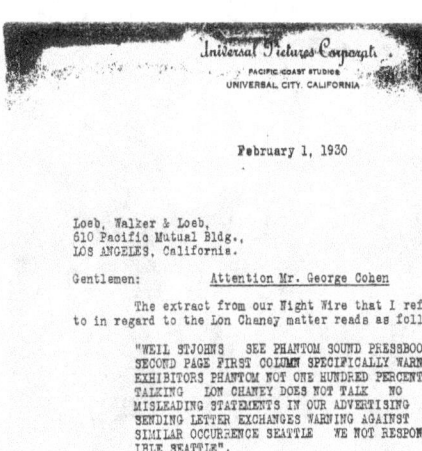

February 1, 1930

Loeb, Walker & Loeb,
610 Pacific Mutual Bldg.,
LOS ANGELES, California.

Gentlemen:    Attention Mr. George Cohen

The extract from our Night Wire that I referred to in regard to the Lon Chaney matter reads as follows:

"WEIL STJOHNS SEE PHANTOM SOUND PRESSBOOK SECOND PAGE FIRST COLUMN SPECIFICALLY WARN EXHIBITORS PHANTOM NOT ONE HUNDRED PERCENT TALKING LON CHANEY DOES NOT TALK NO MISLEADING STATEMENTS IN OUR ADVERTISING SENDING LETTER EXCHANGES WARNING AGAINST SIMILAR OCCURRENCE SEATTLE WE NOT RESPONSIBLE SEATTLE".

Unfortunately, there is no copy of the Press Book in Los Angeles, and we have asked New York to Air Mail one to us.

Yours very truly,

UNIVERSAL PICTURES CORPORATION

W. L. Stern,
Business Manager

WLS:JAB

Above are pages from Chaney's contract with Universal for the 1929 sound reissue of The Phantom of the Opera. So as far as the Phantom was concerned Chaney would allow Universal to use his likeness only, and permission to use a voice double for $25,000 provided that they made no claims to it actually being his voice.

*For more on Lon Chaney see appendix B- A reconstruction of "My Own Story" by Lon Chaney, as close as possible to the original format. It was the only time he ever talked about his formulative years in barnstorming, vaudeville and his earlier years at Universal Pictures. It appeared orginally in a short lived magazine called "Movie Magazine from September to November in 1925*

*Even with the problems with Phantom, Chaney's first talking picture would be released only a few months before his death.*

All this upheaval didn't stop Junior. And by June of 1930 Universal finally bought the rights to film Dracula. Around the same time that Chaney's first and only talking film *The Unholy Three* was released by MGM with tremendous success. Two months later Universal bought the screen rights to Dracula which included a complete print and script of F.W. Murnau's Nosferatu

Famed author Louis Bromfield was given the project of the first treatment with a July deadline. Everything began to look like it would fall in place again so the project was rushed by adding screenwriter Dudley Murphy to complete the screenplay. Universal was going to make in the Super Jewel quality of The *Hunchback of Notre Dame* in 1923 and *The Phantom of the Opera* and they based their script on the book. They knew that Chaney was always more involved when the screenplay was close to the original novels, as was the first version of his Phantom that premiered in Los Angeles, in being very close to the Gaston Leroux novel of 1911.

*Dudley Murphy*

Dudley Murphy was born on July 10, 1897 in Winchester Massachusetts. The son of a Harvard professor, after graduating from M.I.T. he was a journalist and assistant drama editor before turning to films in the early 20s. beginning with a string of one-reelers. In his first short film *Soul of the Cypress (1921)*, a variation on the Orpheus myth, the film's lead falls in love with a dryad (a wood nymph whose soul dwells in an ancient tree) and throws himself into the sea to become immortal and spend eternity with her. Murphy's then -wife Chase Harringdine play the dryad. Murphy followed this with *Danse Macabre* (1922) featuring Adolph Bolm, Olin Howland and Ruth Page. A very eerie film where the lead's girlfriend is being stalked by death in the form of a skeleton.

In 1924 he went to France, where he produced and helped direct Fernand Léger experimental classic *Ballet mécanique*. On returning to the US he wrote a number a screenplays and directed feature films. His work on Dracula is uncredited in the final release.

He moved his production crew to Mexico in the 40s while he and his fourth wife, Virginia still operated an exclusive Malibu hotel which was a favorite of the Hollywood crowd.

He died in Mexico City on February 22, 1968.

Filmography: *The Soul of the Cypress* (1921); *High Speed Lee* (1923); *Ballet mécanique* (1924); *Skyscraper, Alex the Great, Stocks and Blonds* (1928); *St. Louis Blues, Jazz Heaven, Black and Tan, The Burglar* (1929); *Dracula,* (English and Spanish versions) additional dialogue; *He was Her Man, Confessions of a Co-Ed,* (1931); *A Lesson in Golf, The Sport Parade* (1932); *The Emperor Jones* (1933); *The Night is Young,* (1935); *Don't Gamble with Love,* (1936); One *third of a Nation, Main Street Lawyer,*

*Carl Laemmle Sr.*

(1939); *Yes Indeed, Merry-Go-Roundup, Lazy Bones, I Don't Want to Set the World on Fire, Easy Street, Alabamy Bound, Abercrombie Had a Zombie,* (1941); *Yolanda* (1943); *Alma de bronce* (1944).

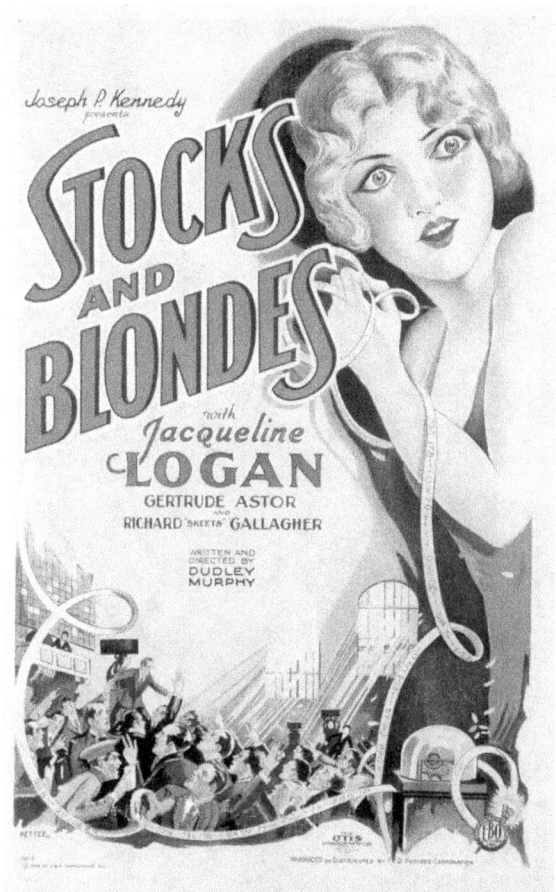

*Louis Bromfield*

Louis Bromfield, (born Louis Brumfield), a Pulitzer Prize winning author, was born December 27, 1896 on a farm in Mansfield, Ohio. He was a direct descendant of American frontiersman Daniel Boone. In addition to his writing career he specialized in the field of scientific farming, writing a number of books on the subject. His own farm Malabar, in Lucas Ohio still exist today as a state park. [The following is from his obituary from the New York Times]

At 18, after a stint on a local newspaper, he enrolled in Cornell School if Agriculture and returned to his family farm after only one semester. After a few months of farming he enrolled in Columbia University's School of Journalism.

With the start of World War I, he left college and joined the French Army as an ambulance driver. He came out of the war with the star of the Legion of Honor and the Croix de Guerre

Mr. Bromfield entered the metropolitan newspaper scene as rewrite man for the old New York City News Association after which he went to The Associated Press. He held several magazine and advertising jobs, and then went to France. There he settled down to a writing career.

His first four novels consisted of panels in the American scene. "The Green Bay Tree" published in (1923) won instant acclaim. There followed "Possession" (1925), "Early Autumn" [Pulitzer Prize winner] (1926) and "A Good Woman" (1927). Thereafter there was a book almost every year.

Mr. Bromfield's novels evolved eventually into sleek Hollywood-slanted stories. The motion picture rights for *Mrs. Parkington* (1943) were sold for $60,000 on the basis of a one-paragraph synopsis before he began writing the book.

After travels and a residence in India, which furnished backgrounds for several more books (Including "The Rains Came" and A Night in Bombay), he returned to Ohio In 1939 and bought his farm where he lived his death on March 18, 1956. His contribution to Dracula are uncredited.

Filmography: *One Heavenly Night, 24 Hours, (1931); Night After Night, (1932); The Life of Vergie Winters, A Modern Hero, (1934); The Rains Came, (1939); Brigham Young, It All Came True, (1940); Johnny Come Lately, (1943); Mrs. Parkington, (1944), The Rains of Ranchipur, (1955)*

FIRST TREATMENT

of


"DRACULA"


By


Louis Bromfield




July 18, 1930

JOHN HARKER

    Young, attractive, romantic barrister, just beginning to practice. He is blonde, blue-eyed, physically strong and perhaps bumptious. He is romantically devoted to his fiancee, Mina Seward.

COUNT DRACULA

    Handsome, dark, tall and slender, almost to the point of thinness, but of super-human muscular strength. He is physically potent and attractive, at times seeming to be perfectly normal. It is only when the lust of blood, or terror of his own destruction seizes him, that he turns sinister. His canine teeth appear visibly to grow longer, and his eyes to dilate. His eyes are all important. They are dark and lustrous with a kind of evil power of hypnotism.

1      EXTERIOR OF AN INN
       In the wildest part of the Transylvanian
       mountains. A low, squalid building, is the
       last stages of decay. It has queer
       sinister angles and long narrow windows.
       It is a winter night in the middle
       of a wild blizzard. The pine trees
       are bowing before the blast. The
       wind howls and once or twice is
       heard the howl of a wolf. Two
       or three of the animals slink across
       the courtyard, circling the inn and
       leaping up to peer in a half-human
       way in at the cracks of the
       shuttered windows. Once or twice
       are heard snatches of savage music
       played by gypsies inside.

2. THE INTERIOR OF BEDROOM
       IN THE LOFT OF THE INN

       It is a long room, barely
       furnished with a bed, a chair,
       a table, and on the floor a
       wolf skin. The room is lighted only
       by the candle on the table.

       Seated there is John Harker. He
       is packed ready for a journey
       his bag beside him. He is warmly
       dressed against the cold, with a
       fur coat and gloves on the table
       beside him. He is writing a letter
       with a fountain pen.

       From belowstairs comes the faint
       sound of a weird, savage, wailing
       music played by the native band.

       The camera looking over his
       shoulder reads:

       "If anything happens to me you
       will know that I came as far as
       Biztritz, safely. I must say
       that as I penetrate further into
       these wild mountains, I begin to
       feel vaguely uneasy, It is like
       going back into the middle ages.
       The country is full of superstition,
       ghosts and tales of men and even
       women who rise from the grave at

                  (CONTINUED)

A-2  CONTINUED

    night to take on the forms of wolves and bats. From here on, I must journey by an means possible. Motors cannot traverse the wild roads. For some reason the natives regard me as a man already doomed. Thank Heaven I am a solid, sensible Britisher not to be frightened by wild tales of horror. Say nothing to Mina of what I have written you. I would not have her frightened for the world." He signs the letter, folds it, places it in an envelope and addresses it to

    "Penthurst, Williams & Harker, Barristers, Fleet Street, London"

    As he folds the letter, the shutter rattles. Pausing, he sits transfixed, staring at it. Then he turns again to write and again the shutter rattles, half rattle, half knock. Stealthily he rises and moving toward it, suddenly opens the window and flings the shutters open. There is nothing there. Below him in the courtyard he sees a wolf sling off into the shadows.

    Closing the shutter, re returns to the desk and starts another letter.

    "Darling Mina:
              Just a line before leaving for Castle Dracula. I shall not be able to write you every day from there. I am well and in fine spirits, though I miss you horribly. The country is interesting and beautiful, though very savage and the trip is fine experiences, although nothing can take the place of you. It won't be long now until we shall never again be separated. My love to your father and to Lucy. If you had not been yourself, I should have fallen in love with her. I am wearing the little crucifix which you gave me. Nothing will ever separate it and me. I hope to finish this mission in short order and then, when I return, you will be my wife.

              Jonathan Harker.

        (CONTINUED)

A-2  (CONTINUED - 2)

    He takes out the crucifix from beneath his shirt and kisses it romantically.

    Again the rattling of the shutters. Again, somewhat terrified, he stares at it. The rattling continues, as if there was an attempt to force an entrance. Slowly he raises the tiny crucifix toward the window, calling out in a loud voice, "Back to the Devil from where you came".

    At once, the rattling ceases and with it the howl of the wind and the wolves.

    Harker smiles a half-credulous smile, seals the envelope, addresses it, picks up his coat and bag and carrying the candle, starts toward the door. The wind begins to howl once more and with the distant howl of the wolves.

A-3  THE DRINKING ROOM OF THE INN

    'It is like the exterior of the house, ancient, crumbling and worn. There is a gigantic fireplace in one corner and in the opposite corner a crazy stairway landing to the rooms above. The whole room is distorted like something seen in a dream.

    In the room are seated, drinking and carousing, a villainous assortment of Transylvanian peasants. In one corner are two or three savage peasants playing the music that has been heard up to now. The proprietor, a lean, sallow fellow of great height and fierce black moustaches, is seated behind a sort of till.

    At the top of the stairs Harker appears. One of the peasants sees him, then another and another. They all stop drinking. The music stops. They all stare at him in pity and terror, as he slowly descends the stairs. One or two cross themselves.

    Harker advances slowly across the room until he reaches the till where he addresses the proprietor.

               (CONTINUED)

A-3     (CONTINUED)

      HARKER
        Has the sleigh come you?

      PROPRIETOR (he speaks English
          with a broad accent)

        No....I think you'll hear
        it when it comes.

      HARKER(handing him the two
         letters)

        When will these go?

      PROPRIETOR

        Day after tomorrow. The
        mail coach only comes into
        the mountains once a week.

      HARKER

        They're important. I
        trust you to see that they
        get off.

      PROPRIETOR

        You can trust me.

      HARKER(looking about at the
         peasants who continue
         to stare at him)

        What's the matter with me?

      PROPRIETOR

        Its because you're a
        stranger, Sir. They have
        never been out of the
        mountains.

      HARKER

        They must be used to me by now.

      PROPRIETOR

        They're very ignorant, Sir.

An old moustached hag
suddenly comes forward
and throws herself at
Harker's feet. She holds
out a charm toward him
and mumbles excitedly in
Czechoslovak.

      HARKER(drawing back,
        Alarmed)
(CONTINUED)       What's the matter? What's
       she saying?

A-3   (CONTINUED - 2)

                     PROPRIETOR

                          Take it.
                                (indicating the object
                                she is holding out)
                          It's a charm against the
                          evil forces

Harker takes it. The old woman, crossing herself, seizes his knees. He frees himself.

                     HARKER

                          What's she saying?

                     PROPRIETOR

                          Perhaps I ought not to tell you.

                     HARKER(angrily)

                          Tell me.  I'm not a fool or a coward.

                     PROPRIETOR

                          I didn't mean that, you Excellency.
                                (hesitating)
                          She is saying that tonight is the Eve of St. George's Day.

                     HARKER

                          Yes!

                     PROPRIETOR   (hesitating)

                          At midnight all the evil things in the world will be loosed.

                     HARKER(laughing)

                          Yes!  And what are they?

Proprietor doesn't answer.

                     HARKER(again)

                          What are they?

                     PROPRIETOR   (evasively)

                          Demons - werewolves - vampires.  It is evil to even speak of them.

             (CONTINUED)

A-3  (CONTINUED - 3)

> HARKER (laughing)
>
> Well, if it's not any more than that, I shan't worry. I fancy I'll be safe in the castle of my friend, Count Dracula. It's walls are thick enough.

The proprietor crosses himself.

> HARKER (looking at him seriously)
>
> What? You believe too?

The clock begins striking midnight slowly.

> PROPRIETOR
>
> You can never tell -- I've seen things --

> HARKER
>
> What things?

> PROPRIETOR (after a pause)
>
> You had better keep the charm the old woman gave you.

> HARKER (laughing)
>
> Our friend, the coachman is late.

> PROPRIETOR
>
> I think he never meant to come before midnight.

The sound of horses' hoofs are heard. They both listen. In the background the peasants grow terrified. A wolf howls. The clock finishes striking. There is a knock, made by the butt of a whip, on the door.

The Proprietor makes no effort to unbolt the door. He has placed himself with his back against the wall, motionless. All the peasants are struck dumb and appear terrified. Harker looks at him and then unbolts the door himself.

(CONTINUED)

A-3   (CONTINUED - 4)

                    HARKER

                         Goodnight. I'll return
                         here when my visit is
                         finished.

                    PROPRIETOR   (in a low voice)

                         May God bring you safely
                         back.

Harker opens the door.
The wind blows in. A
wolf howls. He closes
it and the Proprietor
flings himself on it
bolting it and making
the mark of the cross
in chalk.


A-4   THE COURTYARD AND ROAD
      OUTSIDE THE INN

      It is roughly paved an lighted
      only by the lantern above the
      Inn door.

      As Harker steps to the door under
      the light it is banged behind him.
      In front of him stands a sleigh
      drawn by four coal-black horses
      prancing nervously. For a moment
      he stands taking in the sight and
      then notices the extraordinary
      figure of the coachman.

      He is a big man, wrapped in furs
      with a scarf hiding the lower
      part of his face like a mask,
      beneath the wolf-skin cap. The
      only visible part of his face
      are his eyes, which are large,
      black and brilliant. As they
      regard Harker they seem to
      dilate and take on an expression
      of gloating. For a moment Harker
      stands staring at him with an
      expression of amazement and then
      alarm. The wolves howl louder
      and nearer. Without speaking a
      word Harker climbs into the
      sleigh and is whirled off. At
      the same time the wolves appear
      from the bushes close in pursuit.
      Harker, alarmed, half rises from
      beneath furs which he has thrown
      over himself and drawing his
      pistol turns to face the wolves.
                         (CONTINUED)

A-4    (CONTINUED)

He fires once or twice as they draw near, but the mysterious coachman rising in his seat, turns and cracks his long driving whip in the direction of the wolves, who instantly vanish. Again Harker is both astonished and frightened. The coachman appears to take no notice of the extraordinary happening and Harker settles back as the sleigh dashes on.


A-5    A LONG SHOT OF CASTLE DRACULA

It is an immense and crumbling ruin of the ages, silhouetted against waning moon, which appears now and then thru the storm tormented clouds. The sleigh drawn back by the black horses sweeps into the courtyard, before an immense doorway, which is also a kind of porch where Harker is sheltered from the storm. He gets down from the sleigh again, bearing his luggage and dispatch case. Again no word is spoken between him and the mysterious coachman. Suddenly the sleigh dashes off. Apparently whisked to invisibility by a wild gust of wind and snow. Harker is left alone, standing in the fitful moonlight before the great door.

On the door is an immense iron knocker with which he hammers again and again, against the moldering iron-studded oak. For a long time there is no answer. The wolves begin to howl again, the howling coming nearer and nearer, until, as they rush into the vast courtyard. There is a metallic sound of chains and bolts, the great door opens, apparently of its own accord, and he steps inside and the door closes again. He finds himself confronted by an immensely tall man in old-fashioned, very worn, footman's livery. He silently takes up the baggage of Harker and without a words leads the way. Harker follows.

(CONTINUED)

A-5  (CONTINUED)

    The hallway is an immensely high, narrow, vaulted passageway and is lighted only by the candle-stick, very rich and very beautiful, bearing six candles which the man-servant has given to Harker to carry while he himself brings the baggage. The candle-light throws fantastic shadows against the walls.

    The long hall terminates in an immense stone stairway, which appears to lead up and up indefinitely. It is likewise completely bare and as the two figures climb up and up they grow smaller and smaller, until in a turning of the staircase, they are lost to sight.


A-6  AGAIN AN IMMENSE HIGH VAULTED ROOM WITH SMALL WINDOW ALONG ONE SIDE

    It is dark, except for the moonlight which comes in by a small window... A great door opens and a man-servant comes in followed by Harker carrying the candle-stick, which illuminates the room for the first time. This room, too, is virtually bare, save for a group of furniture, crude and massive, gathered about an immense fireplace filled with burning logs.

    The man-servant leads the way to the fireplace, where he puts down the luggage, bows and goes out without a word. Harker, left alone, takes off his fur coat and looks about him. He notices suddenly that the chairs and table are covered thickly with dust and traces, with his finger a faint design on the surface of the table. On the table lie bread, cheese fruit and a bottle of wine. A place is set for one person. While waiting, he wanders about the room gong presently to one of the windows which he unfastens with difficulty. Opening it he looks out.

A-7   SCENE BENEATH THE WINDOW
      SEEN FROM AN ENORMOUS
      HEIGHT

   Half blotted out by the snow
   lies a mountainous landscape
   threaded by a river. Beneath
   the window there is a sheer
   drop of castle-wall and
   precipice of a thousand feet.
   The wall of the castle is
   broken only by another window
   a hundred feet lower down.


A-8   INSIDE THE ROOM

   Harker draws back from the
   window, dizzy by the great
   height. Behind him the howl
   of wolves is heard. He bangs
   the window shut and a moment
   later a voice is heard coming
   out of the shadows.

                       VOICE
                 It is a long drop
                 nearly two thousand feet.

   Harker, turning toward
   the voice, sees the figure
   of a tall man, dressed in a
   musty and unpressed, trousers
   and morning coat. He has a
   very pale face with drooping
   white mustache and long, unkept
   white hair. Yet he has a
   distinction of bearing. He wears,
   also, a long black cape, which
   floats about him as he moves forward
   to greet Harker.

   As he comes into the firelight
   it is the eyes which Harker sees
   first - large, black and
   burning. Suddenly Harker
   sees, in his mind at the same
   time, the eyes of the wild
   coachman and the sinister
   footman. The eyes of all
   three are the eyes of the
   same man.

                       HARKER
                 Count Dracula?


                (CONTINUED)

A-8     (CONTINUED)

                DRACULA   (he speaks with a foreign accent)

                I am Dracula. I bid you welcome. My servants have gone to bed. Let me see to your comfort myself. I pray you, be seated and sup when you please. Excuse me if I do not join you, I never sup.

They seat themselves and Harker brings out papers and lays them on the table.

                HARKER

                I will present my credentials
                    (taking up dispatch case)
                And I have the leases already to sign.
                    (He brings out the papers)

                DRACULA

                I make my apologies for having brought you all the way from London into this wild country - Please eat, while I talk - -

                HARKER

                I have not much appetite, but I will have a little wine, it will warm me after my journey.

                DRACULA

                Your nerves are shaken by the wild ride. I apologize, it is a wild country.
                    (wolves howling)
                    (Dracula grins showing suddenly two very prominent teeth, very long and pointed.)
                Listen to them - - the children of the night. What music they make.

Dracula sits with his hands on the edge of the table, and all the time he is talking, Harker with an evil fascination, regards them and various features of his face.

                (CONTINUED)

A-8    (CONTINUED - 2)

(All this may be shown in
close-ups in and out of the
speech) One by one Harker
examines them. (1) the hands,
coarse and covered with hair
almost like the bristles of
an animal. The mails are long
and pointed in needle-like
fashion. As one hand turns
over you see hairs growing
out of the palm. (2) the
eyebrows, very dark and bushy.
(3) The ears, very pointed at
the tips with a suspicion of
hair on them.

                        DRACULA

              I was forced to make you
              take this long trip because
              it was impossible for me
              to leave my castle. Now
              it seems, owing to sudden
              developments, I shall be
              able to leave shortly to
              occupy the house you have
              bought for me in England.
                    (he leans toward
                    Harker laying a hand
                    on his shoulder)
              Ah! You are a stout
              young fellow - young and
              full of life. There is
              nothing like youth - youth
              and young blood.
                    (he looks at Harker,
                    who, a little
                    frightened, draws
                    away)
              You are young and full of
              young blood. Yes....yes
              full.
                    (for a moment he seems
                    in a trance. Then
                    he draws away and
                    recovers himself.

              Yes - if you will give me
              the papers, I can sign
              them, now at once. I shall
              be busy during the day
              tomorrow and not able to
              see you. I have the
              necessary checks which I
              can pay you at once.

Harker produces the papers.
Dracula draws over to him an
inkwell with a quill pen and
proceeds to sign. He holds
out the checks.
                (CONTINUED)

A-8    (CONTINUED - 3)

Throughout the scene Count Dracula alternately wavers between behaviour, which is all that is polished and polite, and a sudden sinister, gloating over Harker, which he seems unable to control.

          HARKER (with an air of trying
               to make conversation)

      I trust, Sir, that you will find your stay in England agreeable.

          DRACULA

      It will be a change, I have lived so long in this wild, lonely country -
          (slowly, as if to
            himself)
So long, so many, many, years, and now I'm going to a new, fresh world.
          (slowly)
A world full of opportunity.
          (coming to himself
            again)
You will, I am afraid, be forced to stay here for several days, as there is no coach coming from the village before Friday. I trust you will be able to amuse yourself during the day. I am occupied during the daylight, but I shall be able to see you in the evening.
          (rising)
An now, let me conduct you to your room.

He rises and takes up Harker's baggage. Harker protests, but he insists. Leading the way, Dracula conducts Harker to a door on the opposite side of the room.

A-9 A SMALL ROOM WITH A
SINGLE WINDOW

The window looks out over
the valley. The room is
simply furnished.

The two enter and Dracula,
with an air of a servant
opens Harker's bag on the
bed and begins to unpack
for him.

         DRACULA
         You will allow me, I
         trust, inasuch as all
         the servants are in
         bed.

Harker protests and begins
to unpack himself. Among
other things, he takes out
a large, round shaving
mirror. He turns to hang
it on the wall. Dracula
quietly slips the revolver
he finds in the bag into
his own pocket. Meanwhile
Harker, engaged in hanging
up the mirror, notices
that in it there is no
reflection of Dracula.
Puzzled, he deliberately
holds the mirror so that he
can have in it a full view
of Dracula. To his
astonishment no reflection
of Dracula appears. Dracula,
discovering what he is up to,
leaps toward him, seizes the
mirror and dashes it to bits.

Then, recovering himself
sharply, he becomes suave
and polished once more.

         DRACULA
         I beg you pardon. I have
         an incontrollable hatred
         for all mirrors. They are
         symbols of the vanity of
         mankind.
           (he bows)
         And now, Sir, I will leave
         you. I have only one
         request to make. The post
         in these wild mountains is
         very irregular and uncer-
         tain. I would like to have
         you write three letters --
         one dated the third,
         written from here, saying
         that you have arrived,

(CONTINUED)

A-9    (CONTINUED)

> DRACULA (continued)
>
> are comfortable and well -- one written on the sixth saying that you are leaving and one dated the ninth from Bucharest saying that you are on you way to London.
>
> HARKER
>
> Well, I need not trouble you with that. I can send them myself.
>
> DRACULA (looking at him with sinister meaning)
>
> You under stand it would be much safer if you left them to me.
> (bowing his way out the door)
> I will expect to find the letters tomorrow. Good-night, and may you have pleasant dreams.

He closes the door behind him. The clinking of chains and bolts is heard. Harker rushes instinctively to try the massive door and finds it securely bolted. He is a prisoner. He goes to one window and looks out.

A-10    VIEW OF SHEER WALL AND PRECIPICE

It is the same view of the sheer wall and precipice you have seen before.

A-11    VIEW OF OTHER WINDOW

He rushes across the room to the other window. Here too, the walls fall abruptly to the great courtyard by which Harker has entered a little while ago. In the courtyard there appears to be a great activity.

(CONTINUED)

A-11 (CONTINUED)

    The storm is still raging. But, in the courtyard are two great carts and horses and a number of wild looking gypsies. Some are carrying lighted torches, others are carrying from the depths of the castle, great coffin-shaped boxes, of immense weight, loading them upon the carts. Harker watches for a moment and then closes the window. He tries the door again. Searches for his revolver and finds it missing.


A-12   AN IMMENSE FLIGHT OF STAIRS

    An immense flight of stairs leading down, down, down into the depths of the castle. Dracula, his cloak wrapped about him, bolts the door to the large room where Harker has recently had supper and descends the stairs. The camera follows him on the end of descent until he comes out into an immense vaulted, chapel-like room filled with coffins and tombs. Here, a half dozen wild-looking gypsies are at work shovelling the earth into a coffin-like box. Dracula stands watching them until it is filled and placed on the shoulders of six men who bear it out.


A-13   AGAIN IN HARKER'S ROOM

    He has taken off his collar and put on a dressing gown to make himself comfortable, but has not undressed. Again he goes to the window overlooking the valley and looks out. This time the storm has ceased and in the moonlight appears a cloud of mist, which moves toward him assuming fantastic shapes. He closes the window quickly and turns to his bed and lies down. The mist begins seeping in the cracks of the window and fills the room until nothing in it is visible

(CONTINUED)

A-13 (CONTINUED)

    Then quite slowly it dissolves
    and in the room are three women,
    wild and beautiful, in the
    costumes of three different
    periods of history. Hypnotized,
    Harker on the bed, is unable to
    move. The three women move
    toward his bending over laughing
    in an evil way. One of them
    attempts to bare his throat, but
    at that moment, Dracula himself
    appears suddenly and orders them
    to go, bidding them not to touch
    Harker. He drives them through the
    door which is already bolted and
    disappears. Harker rises , not
    sure whether or not he has been
    asleep and again tries the door,
    which he finds closed. Again
    he goes to the window overlooking
    the valley and opening it looks out.

A-14 ————————————————————

    This time, far below Harker, is an
    extraordinary sight. Dracula, in
    his black cape, comes out of the
    window, headfirst and proceeds to
    climb down the wall head-first,
    edging a little side-wise at times.
    His great black cloak spread out
    about him and clinging to the wall
    like the wings of a bat.

    Harker watches, the calculates for
    a moment the distance from his window
    to the window from which Dracula has
    just disappeared. The he sets to
    work making a rope with the bedclothes
    and this he climbs out of the
    window and makes his way down to the
    lower window, slipping into another
    empty room. Then he goes through
    endless rooms finding his way back,
    at last, to the corridor thru which
    he entered the house. He opens the
    door but as he steps onto the porch
    a score of wolves, all howling, rush
    across the courtyard towards him and
    he slips the bolt into place as they
    leap against the door.

    Wandering back, he comes again to the
    great staircase which leads down, down,
    down into the bowels of the castle.
    On his way down he peers out of one
    of the narrow barred windows and sees
    the sun rising over the mountains.
    Continuing downward he comes at last

(CONTINUED)

A-14 (CONTINUED)

    to chapel-like crypt. There with a candle, he feels his way about. Coming at last to three small tombs in a row. The lids of these have all be tumbled off. As he holds the candle higher he sees in them the three women who have entered his room in the mist. They are lying dead in their coffins. The three tombs each bear birth and death dates that are generations apart, all more than 300 years ago. Beyond them is a more pretentious tomb from which the lid is likewise be lifted. It bears the name "Dracula". and the date 1204 to 1298.

    On the ground all about the tomb are scattered picks and shovels and freshly dug earth.

    In the big tomb lies Dracula himself, wrapped in his black cloak. Harker stares at him for a moment and the seizing one of the shovels, swings it with all his force at the head of the monster. But as he does so the head of the corpse turns over so slightly, the eyes open and fix him with a horrible stare. His arm falters. He drops the spade and turning, runs up the long stairs and down the corridor to the door which unbolts.

    It is daylight now. He runs out into the storm. There are no wolves. He, too, disappears in a great whisp of flying snow.

## SEQUENCE "B"

| | |
|---|---|
| DR. SEWARD | A distinguished man of 50. Proprietor of Carfax Sanitarium for persons with nervous diseases. |
| MINA SEWARD | His daughter, and the fiancee of John Harker. She is young, plump, voluptuous and appetizing. |
| LUCY SEWARD | Also Dr. Seward's daughter. She has once been like Mina, but is now wasted and pale from some mysterious disease which none can diagnose. She is the fiancee of Lord Godalming. |
| MRS. TRIPLETT | A rich neighbor of the Sewards. She is a fat, sill, couquettish woman of about fifty who behaves as if she were still attractive to men. She is a good deal of a fool. |
| COUNT de VILLE | A handsome, youthful foreigner Hungarian in origin - physically attractive to both girls and to Mrs. Triplett. He has beautiful hypnotic eyes which are like the eyes of Dracula. |
| RENFIELD | A patient in Doctor Seward's sanitarium. Thin, gaunt, morbid, about thirty years old. |
| VAN HELSING | A celebrated Dutch Scientist. plump, solid and bearded with an academic manner |

B-1    THE EXTERIOR OF DR. SEWARD'S
       RESIDENCE AND SANITARIUM AT
       CARFAX NEAR LONDON

It is a big, quiet, ivy-grown
house, set in a walled garden,
It is night. By the light above
the gate one can read the digni-
fied brass plate sign.

    CARFAX NURSING HOME
    AND SANITARIUM FOR
    THE CARE OF NERVE
    DISEASES.

    EDWARD SEWARD, ESQ. M.D.

On the wall a sign -

    "LONDON 30 MILES"
    OXFORD 20 MILES, ETC.

A tall man wearing a black
cape approaches, opens the
gate and enters. The Camera
follows him and he approaches
the door, rings and is ad-
mitted. The prolonged howl
of the wolf heard in the
last scene continues until
the door is opened. A servant admits him. The camera
follows him into the drawing room.

The drawing room is a large
comfortable room with tall
curtained windows. In the
center of the room some
people are playing bridge -
Dr. Seward, a thin nervous
man of about 50 with grey-
ing hair. His daughter Mina,
a pretty, voluptuous young
woman who is John Harker's
fiancee, Lord Godalming,
fiancee of Mina's sister,
Lucy and Mrs. Triplett
(Alison Skipworth) a woman
of fifty, but coquettish
and rather silly. She is a
neighbor who can play bridge
and has forced them into a
game. As the servant announces
the Count de Ville, they all
turn toward the door where
the man in the cape still
stands with his back to the camera.

The four faces at the bridge
table register various ex-
pressions - Mr. Triplett,
coquettish and beaming with
delight, Dr. Seward polite
interest, Ford Godalming the
same. Only Mina betrays herself for a moment by a look
of horror. Dr. Seward and Lord
Godalming rise from their
chairs.

B-2  DR. SEWARD GREETING
     COUNT de VILLE

As Doctor Seward rises to greet the Count de Ville you see the Count for the first time. He is Dracula, but miraculously altered. His hair and moustache instead of being grey, are black. He appears young, very good looking vigorous and attractive. There is only a shade of the sinister in him, which appears to expand wherever his gaze is turned toward the pretty voluptuous Mina.

After the greetings are exchanged, he says he has dropped in for a moment to inquire about Lucy. Dr. Seward says she is about the same, very pale and very weak, and in a sort of coma. Dr. Seward tells him that both he, and Lord Godalming have submitted to trans fusions in order to help her condition. The Count gallantly offers himself in case of another transfusion. He asks if she is well enough to receive visitors and is told that she is too weak, although Dr. Seward says that she always seems brighter and more cheerful after seeing the Count. The Count says that he will go now and not interrupt their bridge, but Mina, politely says it does not matter, because she can't possibly go on playing. they had been playing simply to pass the time, and because Mrs. Triplett dropped in and wanted a game. She says she is too sad and depressed to go on pretending she is enjoying it. Mrs. Triplett asks the Count if he will drop her at home. She has walked over from her house. He gallantly agrees, and as they go out, the Count manages to take Dr. Seward aside and ask if there is any news of Miss Mina's fiance, John Harker. He confides in the Count that he is afraid some fatal accident has happened to him. It is three months since they have heard from him. The Count expresses sympathy, and conducts the twittering Mrs. Triplett out of the house. On the (CONTINUED)

B-2    (CONTINUED)

    way out he turns and asks "When is your friend Van Helsing, arriving?" Dr. Seward says "we expect him tonight." An then looking sharply at the Count asks, "how did you know that he was coming?" The Count replies. I heard you speaking of it the other day".

    Back in the drawing room Mina is very nearly hysterical. She declares she cannot bear the Count, and that his presence near her, fills her with dread. Dr. Seward admits there is something strange about him. How does he know that Van Helsing is on his way from Amsterdam. He is certain that the subject was never discussed in front of him. At that moment a maniacal laugh is heard. Mina very nearly faints. Lord Godalming snatches away the curtain and standing there , jeering at them is discovered Renfield, a patient in the sanitarium.

    Dr. Seward, alarmed, asks him what he is doing there and bids Godalming to ring the bell for the keeper at once. From Renfield comes only insane chatter. He is at the moment, completely mad. The keeper appears to drag Renfield away and Renfield makes a speech begging to be allowed a single night of freedom. He is hysterical and pitiful. Dr. Seward, to humor him, tells him "yes, but later on". Renfield, jibbering to himself is dragged away by the keeper. As he leaves the room he emits a long wolf-like howl. The howl is answered distantly from the outside. Godalming observes that Renfield has started all the dogs in the neighborhood to howling.

    Godalming urges Dr. Seward to send Renfield away because he is growing violent and his screams and yells must be disturbing to the sick Lucy. Mina leaves them, saying that she is going up to see her sister, Lucy, and as she leaves a servant enters bringing the mail. There is a letter bearing the stamp of John Harker's law firm. Seward opens it hastily hoping that perhaps it may contain news of John Harker. Godalming watches while he reads.

B-3   LUCY'S BEDROOM

It is an old-fashioned room with a low dormer window looking out on the park. It is moonlight and the room is lighted only by the window and a night light. The door opens and Mina comes in. She moves softly to the foot of the bed and stands for a moment looking down at her sister.

Lucy, lying on the bed, looks pale and shaken. She is wearing a bed-jacket and a scarf wrapped around her throat. The is moaning in her sleep and talking to herself. Presently she opens her eyes and recognizes her sister, who falls on her knees beside the bed and takes Lucy in her arms, asking her how she feels. Lucy in a daze, answers her brokenly. Suddenly, with an odd look of unearthly joy, she points to the window and says, "look, there he is, come back. Let him in." Turning, Mina sees against the window pane the outline of a huge bat.

Mina regards the sight with horror and taking up a candlestick as a weapon advances toward the window. Courageously she opens the window. As she does the bat flies off into the moonlight. Closing the window Mina bolts it firmly.

Returning to the bed she finds that Lucy has slipped into unconsciousness again. She does not rouse her. There is a knock and Lord Godalming advances and says softly, "John has been found." She asks fearfully if he is alive and he says: "Yes". He draws her outside the door where he tells her the truth and hands her the letter. "John", he says, "is on his way home. He will arrive in two weeks." While she reads the letter he goes inside and bending over, kisses Lucy's hand gently. Lucy stirs, wakens and looking at Lord Godalming cries out, "No - don't touch me! I'm unclean! Go! - - Leave me in peace!" She sinks back again on the bed, unconscious.

(CONTINUED)

B-3     (CONTINUED)

While they are bending
over her the long howl
of dogs is heard again.
They turn fearfully to-
wards the window. The
outline of a bat is seen
there again. Again Godalming
goes to the window and frightens
away the bat, which flies out
into the moonlight. Again they
bolt the window and this time
draw the curtains across it
shutting out the moonlight.

Godalming beckons silently
for Mina to leave the room.
They go out quietly, closing
the door after them.


B-4     THE HALLWAY OUTSIDE LUCY'S BEDROOM

Godalming says that he is
going with his rifle to shoot
the cursed bat. He is one
of the best shots in England
and cannot miss it. Mina
says she will remain outside
the door. She takes Harker's
letter from her pocket and
begins to read it all over
again.


B-5     THE DRAWING ROOM AGAIN

A servant enters and
announces Dr. Van Helsing.
The Doctor comes in and
between him and Seward
there is a warm greeting.

                    DR. SEWARD

                        Thank God, you've come.
                        I'm at my wits end. We
                        cannot discover what is
                        wrong with Lucy. She
                        grows weaker every day,
                        and has all the symptoms
                        of anemia. But when her
                        blood is analyzed it is
                        normal. We have given
                        her three infusions -
                        gallons of blood, but it
                        has simply vanished.

Van Helsing says that all
the details of the case
fascinate him. He has
many theories, none of
which he will discuss now.
He is very grave and
                                        (CONTINUED)

B-5    (CONTINUED)

    mysterious about the disease.

    A howl is heard. Van Helsing listens for a moment with an expression of deep interest, and then says in a low voice, "the howl of a wolf. Have you a caged wolf in the park?"

                  SEWARD

                      No - that is one of the patients. A man called Renfield. Lately he has taken to howling like that.

                  VAN HELSING

                      No living man ever made that sound.

                  SEWARD

                      You shall see for yourself. I will take you to see him. He is a most interesting case. What is described as zoo-aphagous. He tries to eat life by eating spiders and flies and even sparrows which he lures to his room.

                  VAN HELSING          (gravely)

                      I should, indeed, like to see him. Indeed I think it will be necessary.

B-6    UPSTAIRS IN THE HALLWAY

    Mina, lying on the sofa reading. Presently, she hears low moans from Lucy's room and rising, she goes slowly to open the door. Softly so as not to disturb Lucy. As she opens the door a look of frightful terror crosses her face. She screams and falls in a faint.

    As she faints in the doorway, Dracula, emerging from the room seizes her, carries her inside and locks the door

                  (CONTINUED)

B-6   (CONTINUED)

    Then with a look of obscene and loathsome gloating he seizes her unconscious body, presses back her head, kisses her passionately, and baring her throat presses his mouth to it with an unholy passion.

    (N.B In his unnatural unearthly manifestations the Count de Ville assumes the insane wolfish appearance of Dracula. His eyes grow dilated and his canine teeth appear to grow much longer.)

    The howl of Renfield is heard again, and then cries of "Lucy" and "Mina" are heard and a pounding on the door.

B-7   OUTSIDE THE DOOR AGAIN

    Van Helsing and Seward trying desperately to enter. They smash open the door with a chair and as they enter a pistol shot is heard outside.

B-8   INSIDE THE ROOM

    Lucy lies on the bed, unconscious, the scarf torn from her throat, On the floor, partly lying on the sofa, lies Mina in the same condition. A wisp of mist seems to hang about the locked and curtained window. Van Helsing and Seward bend over Mina, trying desperately to rouse her. Slowly she comes to, saying: "Where am I? What has happened?" Then hysterically, "go to Lucy - save Lucy."

    Dr. Seward goes to Lucy and Van Helsing bends over Mina, lifting her up and speaking to her.

                    VAN HELSING
            Save her from what?
            Speak to me! From What?
            From what? What have
            you seen? What was it?

    Mina only moans and murmurs "I don't know - I don't know."

B-9    A CORNER OF THE PARK
       SURROUNDING THE SANITARIUM

Again the figure of
the Count di Ville, in
a long cape, is seen
advancing in the moonlight
under the trees. On
the door stop he en-
counters Lard Godalming
carrying a rifle. The
Count bows gravely.

          COUNT    (with a sinister
                      smile)

          Shooting at night, Lord
          Godalming

          GODALMING

          I was trying to get a
          bat which has been
          annoying Miss Seward,
          by trying to enter her
          room. I shot at it and
          I'm sure I hit it, but
          it did not fall. I
          searched everywhere.

          COUNT    (awed)

          A bat at this time of the
          year! Possibly it came
          from Carfax Abbey. The
          old ruin is filled with
          bats.

          GODALMING

          Will you come in and have
          a drink before going to
          bed?

          COUNT

          I meant to drop in. As
          I was passing I heard a
          scream. I thought it
          might have something to
          do with Miss Lucy.

          GODALMING    (in wild alarm)

          A scream! Miss Lucy!
          I heard nothing. Oh,
          my God!

He turns and runs toward
the house. The Count
follows him slowly.

B-10   AGAIN THE DRAWING ROOM

As Godalming rushes into the room still carrying the rifle, a servant, in agitation rushes to him and tells him that something has happened in Miss Lucy's room. Godalming rushes up the stairs and as he exits the Count, still in the cape, crosses the room slowly.

B-11   LUCY'S BEDROOM

Mina lies on the sofa with her head in the pillow, sobbing hysterically. Seward and Van Helsing bend over Lucy.

          VAN HELSING  (rising slowly)

            I have come too late, and only a moment too late. She is dead.

Van Helsing bends down and peers, with a magnifying glass, at Lucy's throat. There are two small marks like the teeth-marks of a bat. He draws back slowly and says: "I was afraid I might find those marks".

Godalming enters. Dr. Seward rises and breaks the news to him. He becomes almost hysterical and kneels by the bed, kissing Lucy's hand and begging her to speak to him.

The Count appears in the doorway, bows, expresses his sympathy and begs pardon for the intrusion. Van Helsing turns and sees him. For a second in close-ups he and the Count regard each other with a long, fixed and hostile look.

The Count begs them to call upon him if there is anything he can do to help. As he bows his way out, the howl of Renfield is heard again

          VAN HELSING (gravely
            That is the howl of no living man.

B-12　AGAIN THE FIGURE OF THE
　　　COUNT IN THE CAPE

　　　Moving under the tree.
　　　This time toward the
　　　Carfax Abbey, the ruin
　　　where he lives. It is
　　　dawn. The sun is
　　　rising. He approaches
　　　a great studded iron
　　　door, and as he advances
　　　toward it the door swings
　　　back of its own accord.
　　　He enters a vaulted stone
　　　hallway. The door closes
　　　behind him and he bolts
　　　and chains it and picking
　　　up a candle, advances
　　　along the corridor to a
　　　stair-way which, like the
　　　great stairway in Castle
　　　Dracula, appears to descend
　　　down and down into the
　　　bowels of the earth. He
　　　disappears from sight
　　　around a turn in the
　　　stairway.

SEQUENCE "C"

C-1    AGAIN THE DRAWING ROOM
OF DR. SEWARD'S NURSING
HOME.

In the room are Lord Godalming, Dr. Seward and Van Helsing. Dr. Seward is dressed in black clothes. Godalming in a grey suit with a black mourning band on his arm. Van Helsing is in an old rumpled tweed suit. All three look worn, distracted and weary.

In a three-cornered conversation Van Helsing slowly explains to them the real cause of Lucy's illness and death. They are incredulous and he at last convinces them that the menace with which they are dealing is no earthly one.

In the middle of the conversation Mina enters. She looks pale and worn and sinks into a chair with weariness. She also is in mourning, dressed to go out and wears about her throat a scarf.

She is going to meet Harker, her fiance, at the railway station. He is returning, having lost his memory, to try to take up again the threads of a life which is already dead.

Dr. Seward protests also, but points out that the greatest danger lies in her going out of doors after nightfall. Mina, however, insists. She points out that the meeting will also be painful for Harker and that she loves him so deeply that she wants their first meeting to be alone. Perhaps, she says, the sight of her will bring back his memory. Van Helsing says that perhaps she is right, but he insisted upon her wearing about her throat, underneath the scarf, a wreath of wolfsbane, which he says, half in jest, is a partial cure for her illness.

(CONTINUED)

C-1    (CONTINUED)

She must, he says,
never go anywhere without
it until she has recovered.
He suddenly grows very
serious about it.
She sets off alone in the
motor for the station.

When she has gone the
conference continues.
Van Helsing explains that
he has sent to Russia
by telegram, for the wolfsbane, which has just arrived. The
smell of it is reputed
to be abhorred by the evil
forces with which they are
beginning to battle. Van
Helsing says that the battle
will be a terrific one and they
will need all the help
possible against the terrific
forces arrayed against them.

Godalming suggest that they
enlist the advice and aid of
Count de Ville, the friend
and neighbor, inasmuch as the
Count comes from Hungary where
the legends and traditions of the
forces they are fighting is
centered. Dr. Seward supports
him, but Van Helsing is doubtful.
He has, he says, suspicions of
the Count and does not wish to call
in his aid until he has tried him
by a proof which he has planned.
Van Helsing says that their first
stop must be to question the
maniac, Renfield, and try to get
at the root of the strange
transforation which has taken
place in his character. He points
out that it began at the
same time as Miss Lucy's illness,
and that both things may be due to
the presence in the neighborhood
of the same evil spirit.

Dr. Seward rings for the keeper
and bids him send for Renfield.

C-2    A CORNER OF THE RAILWAY
       STATION AT CARFAX VILLAGE

The train arrives and John
Harker descends from it.
He is shockingly altered
in appearance, looking older
nervous, and with streaks of white
in his dark hair. He gets down
from the train and looks about
him. Mina comes toward him full
of delight and joy, but he only stares
blankly at her until she says she is
Mina Seward. Then he knows that
this is the girl to whom he was
engaged before his mind went blank.    (CONTINUED

C-2    (CONTINUED

She conducts him to the automobile and they get in and drive away. There is a touching love scene between them in which Mina tries desperately to make him remember all that has passed between them and in which he desperately and shyly, tries to behave as he should toward her. And although he is attracted to her, and in a way in love with her at first sight, he cannot quite feel at ease with a woman who is almost a stranger to him. They begin slowly to come together into an understanding.


C-3    THE DRAWING ROOM AGAIN

Renfield is brought in by his keeper and questioned by Van Helsing. At first he answers sensibly and then slowly he begins to talk jibberish about the presence of "the master". He again begs Dr. Seward to let him free for a single night. He will, he says, return again.. on his word of honor. Dr. Seward says he will allow him freedom if he will speak openly of what he knows. He begins to speak revealing more than he should in hope of saving his soul. While he is speaking a bat flies in at the window, circles the room and goes out. At once Renfield falls hysterically upon his knees, addressing the air as "Master", begging for mercy and declaring that he has betrayed nothing. He becomes completely mad and is lead away by the keeper.

No sooner has he gone than Van Helsing says he is convinced that there is some close relationship between Renfield and the force they are battling.

The same moment Mina and John Harker come in from the station. She seems happy and slushed, but John is still puzzled, as he recognizes neither Dr. Seward nor Godalming, and has, of course never seen Van Helsing. Mina says that now John has returned everything will be alright and that she will recover, but Van Helsing only shakes his head and says that it will not be as easy as that and that she must still obey his smallest instructions.
                    (CONTINUED

49

C-3    (CONTINUED)

    She must wear the herbs about her throat and must never leave the house alone after nightfall, nor be alone for an instant. He summons her maid and tells her that she must never, under any circumstances leave Miss Mina alone. The maid promises.

    The Count de Ville is announced suddenly and Van Helsing says to have him come in. He enters as usual, suave and charming and inquires after Mina's health. He is of course, introduced to John Harker. Harker, of course, does not fathom. There is an awkward moment while they stare at each other and the Count clearly attempts some hypnotic power.

    Then he recovers himself and says that he must be off, as he is leaving for London by the ten O'clock train. Van Helsing suddenly asks him if he will not dine and play bridge on the following evening. The Count hesitates and then replies that he will be delighted. All the while Harker regards him like a bird fascinated with a snake. The Count leaves and when he has gone Harker putting his hands over his eyes groans and says that he know the face and the eyes from somewhere, but can remember nothing.

    Mina tries to comfort him tenderly and says that he ought to retire and lie down for a time before dinner.

    Mina, accompanied by the maid, goes out with John to show him his room. Again, for an instant there is a love scene between John and Mina in the corridor in which John kisses her. John tires desperately to find his way back to the memory of what happened before he wakened in the Transylvania Hospital.

C-4    THE GUEST ROOM

    Mina shows John the room, arranges the flowers, does everything to make him comfortable. She says, she too, is exhausted, and when John questions her about her illness and how pale she looks, she replies evasively and says that

(CONTINUED)

C-4  (CONTINUED)

    it is nothing, and says that she will go now and lie down for a while. While they are talking a lone howl is heard Harker, alarmed, asks what it is. Mina, affected, is forced to sit in a chair.

    A strange look comes over her face and she replies, with some effort, that it si only the howling of the maniac, Renfield. She rises slowly and tells John that she will see him at dinner and leaves the room. On the way out she pauses for a moment as if overcome by dizziness. When she recovers herself she bids the maid go downstairs and fetch her a book from the library, which she describes.

    The maid protests that she has been ordered not to leave her. Mina, outside Harker's door, becomes like a person possessed with a strange craftiness, says that she will wait here until the maid returns. The maid goes. There is again a lone howl, and Mina, as if hypnotized, moves down the corridor out of sight.

C-5  AGAIN THE DRAWING ROOM

    Downstairs, the fat, silly, Mrs. Triplett arrives. Van Helsing explains to her that they asked her to come in on her way home from London because there were questions they desired to ask her about the Count de Ville, who occupies the semi-ruin on the edge of her estate, known as Carfax Abbey.

    She is very coy about the Count, and hints that there is a romantic attachment between herself and him. Van Helsing, however, keeps her to the point and questioning her finds out a great many interesting facts about the mysterious de Ville.

(CONTINUED)

C-5     (CONTINUED)

        She has leased the place
        to him for 99 years in order
        to raise money for the
        income tax. It was all ar-
        ranged by lawyers. She did
        not see him until he called
        on her the day of his arrival.
        The house, she explains, had not
        been occupied for nearly 80
        years; ever since her grand-
        father's time. Most of it was
        a ruin. In the part that was
        livable there was a little
        furniture. The Count did not
        object to this. There was, how-
        ever, a stipulation in the
        lease that so long as he lived
        the place was not to be visited
        by the proprietor or any other
        person without his express
        permission.


C-6     THE BLOOMY PARK BETWEEN
        DR. SEWARD'S SANITARIUM
        AND CARFAX ABBEY

        The Count, wrapped in his
        cloak, stands in the shadow
        of a tree. Thru the trees
        approaches the figure of
        a woman. As she comes nearer she
        turns out to be Mina
        wrapped in a coat. She is
        walking in a perfectly
        straight line with the same
        queer hypnotic look in her
        eyes. The Count de Ville in
        his long black cape, follows
        her at a little distance.
        He comes nearer and nearer
        to her.


C-7     THE DRAWING ROOM AGAIN

        Mrs.; Triplett still being
        questioned by Van Helsing.
        He asks her if she has ever
        noticed anything unusual
        about Carfax Abbey. She
        answers that the only unusual thing seems to be that
        there are no servants and
        that no furniture has ever
        been moved in, unless it came
        in the coffin-shaped boxes which
        she saw arrive one afternoon
        while she was riding thru
        her own park.              (CONTINUED

C-7   (CONTINUED)

   At the mention of the
   boxes, Van Helsing be-
   comes greatly excited, and
   presses Mrs. Triplett
   further. She says they
   appeared to be very heavy
   and it required several men to
   lift them. Her gardener, who talked
   to the carters who brought the
   boxes, aid the boxes were
   labelled "earth for experimental
   purposes."

C-8   THE HALLWAY OUTSIDE HARKER'S
      DOOR.

   The maid approaches
   without the book. She listens
   for a moment at Harker's door,
   then knocks. Harker, himself,
   opens the door and when she
   asks if he knows where Miss
   Mina is, he says he does not.
   Alarmed, they both start to
   search the house. The
   maid will go to Mina's room and
   Harker is to search elsewhere.

C-9   A CORNER OF THE BLOOMY PARK

   Mina, still in a hypnotic
   trance, moves forward as the
   Count comes out of the shadow.
   In a strange voice she addresses
   him as "Master". In a dreadful
   love scene he reproaches her
   for yielding to the advice of
   his enemies and begs her to
   remove from about her throat
   the circlet of wolfsbane. She
   obeys him and he kisses her
   passionately. The scene cul-
   minates and he bares her
   throat and presses his mouth
   against it.

C-10  DRAWING ROOM AGAIN

   The maid, hysterical, rushes
   in and explains that Mina
   is missing. There is great
   confusion and they all rush
   out to search the park, with
   Mrs. Triplett left astonished
   and alone.

C-11  THE PARK OUTSIDE

They are all searching frantically thru the shrubbery under the gloomy trees, calling out Mina's name. It is John Harker who comes upon Mina lying across a bench, unconscious, in the moonlight. As he discovers her, a bat flies up, circles about and vanishes in the moonlight. Again there are three long wolf-howls. John Harker, picking up Mina is joined by the others and they bear her back into the house.

C-12  THE OPERATING ROOM
OF THE SANITARIUM

Godalming, Van Helsing, Dr. Seward and Harker all enter. Mina is placed on the operating table and examined by the two doctors, who say "thank God, it is not too late. "But she must have a transfusion at once." John Harker at once offers himself. Van Helsing says he must see Renfield at once, and bids Seward to take charge of the transfusion while he interviews the maniac.

C-13  A LONG CORRIDOR WITH PRIVATE
ROOMS FOR PATIENTS SUFFERING
FROM NERVE DISEASE, OPENING ON
EITHER SIDE

At one end the keeper sits at a desk asleep. His head on his arm. Van Helsing, in great excitement, rouses him and asks him to open the door of Renfield's padded room. The keeper says that Renfield has been very quiet all evening, not a sound from him. They peer in the small grating of the door and call out his name, but there is no answer. They open the door quickly. Inside it is dark. The keeper, using an electric torch, searches the room. It is in dreadful disorder with the furniture smashed and splintered.
A dreadful sight meets their eyes. Partly on the cot, and in a

(CONTINUED)

C-13  (CONTINUED)

    pool of blood, lies the mangled body of Renfield. Van Helsing cries out, "help me drag the poor devil into the light".

    They drag him into the corridor where Van Helsing makes a hasty examination. He exclaims "his back and neck are broken". "This is the work of a fiend". Renfield, still conscious opens his eyes and murmurs, "Master, I have not betrayed you," and dies. Van Helsing goes at once to the telephone at the end of the corridor and asks for the railway station. There he questions the station-master. "Has the Count de Ville, who lives at Carfax Abbey, taken the train for London?' The station master replies that he left on the train at 9:30, he himself saw him get aboard. Van Helsing hangs up the telephone receiver baffled.

C-14  THE OPERATING ROOM AGAIN

    Godalming, Dr. Seward and John Harker are gathered about Mina. She is slowly regaining consciousness. Van Helsing enters and observes that she is all right and has regained consciousness. He again says that she must not be left alone for an instant and that they each must take turns to keep watch over her, day and night. He proceeds to make a wreath of wolfsbane which he fastens about her throat and then takes from his pocket a small black velvet bag from which he extracts a wafer. Breaking off a piece of it he fastens it with surgical gauze about her throat. Godalming ask him what it si and he replies that "it is the Host". I have a dispensation. Against it all the forces of evil have no power, but we must watch her lest he induces her to remove it.

    He replaces the remains of the waifer in the black sack and puts it in the pocket over his heart.

(CONTINUED)

C-14 (CONTINUED)

    John Harker, in excitement, begs him to tell him the truth and says what is it that is destroying Mina. Van Helsing replies that he must have faith and that tomorrow they will perhaps know the truth. The thing they are fighting is more powerful than all of them together. They must not let it gain an advantage by acting before they are sure of themselves. John Harker, despite his weakened condition, insists upon sitting up all night to guard Mina.

C-15 AGAIN DR. SEWARD'S DRAWING ROOM

    A bridge game is in progress. At the table are seated the Count, Dr. Seward, Mrs. Triplett and Lord Godalming. The Count and Mrs. Triplett are partners. Beside them is a chaise lounge. On it reclines Mina dressed in a negligee with a scarf wrapped about her throat. She looks feeble and ill. Beside her on the chaise lounge sits John Harker. On the other side of the table sits Van Helsing. They all are watching the game.

    As the dialogue develops, it proves that the Count is an uncanny player, that he not only plays expertly, but reads the minds of the other players and has a hypnotic influence on the silly Mrs. Triplett, his partner. Presently John Harker gives a word of advice regarding a play to Mrs. Triplett, at which the Count looks at him with sudden alarm and says: "I thought you didn't play bridge. How do you know about that play?

    Harker replies : I used to know how to play before I was ill, and forgot everything. It is slowly coming back to me. I am beginning to remember fragments of all sorts of things." The game proceeds but the Count still watches Harker with fear

(CONTINUED)

C-15 (CONTINUED)

and suspicion. The Count is now playing a hand and in close-ups, Harker becomes fascinated by the Count's peculiar hands. The are, as in the first sequence, claw-like with fearful cruel nails and covered with wolfish black hair. Something begins to dawn slowly in Harker's mind. Presently one hand of the Count rests on the table, palm up, and Harker see the black hairs growing on the palm. He presses his hands to his head trying vaguely to recall where he had seen this before.

The rubber is finished and Mrs. Triplett takes out her vanity case to powder her nose. The holds in her hand a small square mirror. Suddenly, with a stealthy movement Van Helsing takes the mirror from her and holds it up opposite the Count. In the mirror there is no reflection. The Count turns very slowly, catches Van Helsing making the test, and seizes the hand holding the mirror in his own claw-like paw. In his grasp the mirror is shattered and cuts Van Helsing's hand. At sight of the blood the Count becomes transformed suddenly into Dracula, with fangs and wolflike ears. At sight of him Mina screams and faints recognizing in him the creature who visits her in the night. He leaps to attack Van Helsing, as John Harker, with a look of revelation on his face cries, "Dracula". Everything has come back to him.

Van Helsing snatches from his pocket the black velvet bag containing the "Host" and holding it before him, forces Dracula, still snarling, step by step backward toward the window, crying out "begone Monster!" Dracula passes thru the closed and curtained window and vanishes.

Mrs. Triplett screams and covers her face with her hands.

John Harker, his memory restored in a flash, now recognizes Mina as his fiancee and remembers all his love for her. (CONTINUED)

57

C-15  (CONTINUED) -2

He attempts to raise her from the sofa in his arms and is about to kiss her when she opens her eyes, and cries "No! No! You must not kiss me! I am unclean!" Van Helsing seizing Harker, exclaims - - "She is right, you must not!"

They bring Mina to her senses and as they do so she sees John and recognizes him and says: "Poor John" and strokes his head with her hand. Then she takes from her bosom a newspaper clipping which she silently hands to Van Helsing, who reads it.

It is the strange account of a happening in Bloomsbury, where, on several occasions, small children have been lured, by what they describe " a beautiful lady". After being missing for some hours they have returned, bearing on their throats two small marks, apparently like the marks on the throat of Lucy and Mina.

Van Helsing finishes reading the article and murmurs, "So soon". Mina covers her face with her hands. As Dr. Seward reads the clipping Godalming exclaims with horror, "it is not true - - such things cannot be." Van Helsing replies: "I fear it is Lucy, but there is a way to discover. We will go to the graveyard at dawn. If it is Lucy we shall see her return to her tomb".

Mina, half hysterical, exacts from them the promise that they will tell her nothing of their plans. She and Van Helsing explain that already she is partially in the power of Dracula, and that thru her he can learn of their attempts to destroy him.

Dr. Seward takes Mina away leaving Mrs. Triplett and the three men alone. Mrs. Triplett, hysterical, says she will now return to her own house and Van Helsing bids her stay and guard Mina, while they carry out the work which must be done. She goes to join Dr. Seward and Mina.

(CONTINUED)

C-15   (CONTINUED)-3

    John Harker takes a drink to give him strength to go on with the story of what happened to him in Transylvania, which he now remembers. He begins to recount it to Van Helsing and Godalming.


C-16   THE HALLWAY

    Mrs. Triplett making her way upstairs towards Mina's room. She hears steps coming along the corridor and hides herself, in terror, in an alcove. At the same moment the howl of a wolf is heard. The steps come nearer and it turns out to be only the keeper. She calls out to him and begs him to accompany her to Mina's room. She is too terrified to go alone. As they enter the room Dr. Seward orders the keeper, a burly fellow, to sit up with Mina and Mrs. Triplett. Mina is on the bed but not sleeping. She can no longer sleep at nights, but only sleeps in the daytime. At that moment a sound is heard at the window and looking toward it they see the outline of a great bat against the moonlight. They fling open the window and the keeper fires at it with his pistol and as he hits it, it turns into a cloud of mist.


C-17   THE DRAWING ROOM AGAIN

    John Harker is finishing his story. He says :I raised the spade to crush his head and the corpse turned in the coffin and stared at me. After that I can remember nothing." Van Helsing says: "The boxes are the same as those described by Mrs. Triplett. They are the earth to which the vampire must return at sunrise. We must find them and in one of them, after sunrise, Dracula is certain to be found. If they find him thus he will be helpless. They can then drive a stake thru his heart and destroy him forever."

    Van Helsing has obtained Holy Water to sprinkle upon the earth in each of the boxes.

(CONTINUED)

C-17    (CONTINUED)

        if this is done the vampire cannot return to them.

        Dr. Seward comes in and Van Helsing bids them prepare for the expedition to search for the boxes in haunted Carfax Abbey. Godalming suggests a pistol, but Van Helsing points out that these would be of no use. Instead he gives them each a fragment of the "Host" to wear in a pocket against their hearts. It is no use trying to capture Dracula until sunrise, as he will not return to his box of earth until then.

        He says that before then they must go to the graveyard and wait to see whether Lucy returns to her tomb. If they discover that she is still "Undead" they must, likewise put her at peace by driving a stake thru her heart.

C-18    THE ANCIENT CHURCHYARD WHERE LUCY IS BURIED

        The four men enter thru the gateway among the tombstones. Again there is a howl of a wolf, and in the darkness are seen the burning eyes of scores of animals which appear to have no bodies. The four men plan their action in entering Carfax Abbey and searching it, and as they are talking Van Helsing cries out suddenly -"Look - - it is true". Thru the trees, among the tombs, appears the figure of Lucy. She is dressed all in white, but is transparent and is carrying something in her arms. They watch her with a horrible fascination. Van Helsing restrains Godalming, who starts to cry out and to go forward. Lucy puts down what she is carrying beside a grave-stone and moves on, vanishing suddenly thru the closed door of the tomb.

        The four men advance toward the tomb in which the ghostly figure of Lucy has just entered. Van Helsing takes a key and unlocks the door, saying, "Come, now we shall have the final proof."

                        (CONTINUED)

C-18 (CONTINUED)

    Godalming is overcome and John Harker says, "do not ask this dreadful thing of him". Van Helsing answers that he may wait outside with Dr. Seward. If John Harker will accompany him and do what they must do. John replies that he will do anything that will save Mina, or anything which will save the soul of poor Lucy. They go inside.

C-19 INSIDE THE TOMB

    The only illumination comes from the electric torches which they carry, and from the blow-torch which Van Helsing has with him and which he lights. Then he unscrews the top of the coffin and rips open the lead covering. By the light of the electric torch they discover Lucy lying unchanged, looking perfectly alive. John Harker exclaims "she is not dead, she is living." To which Van Helsing replies, "Nothing can restore her to life. She is one of the undead. There is only one way to save her soul and give her peace. Are you strong enough to help me?"

    Harker, after a moment of hesitation and horror, replies that he is. Van Helsing, taking up the sharpened stake they have brought with them, begins charring the end of it.

C-20 OUTSIDE THE TOMB

    Seward and Godalming wait for the dreadful sound which will mean the end of the gruesome task performed by Van Helsing and Harker. The red eyes of phantom wolves still glimmer in the graveyard and now and then a howl is heard. Suddenly they hear a child crying. Following the sound a little way they come upon a small child lying beside a tombstone. Picking it up they carry it back to the door of the tomb, where Dr. Seward tries to comfort it.

(CONTINUED)

C-20    (CONTINUED)

> There is no especial dramatic value in using the child. On the contrary, it rather clutters up the action and may annoy the censors.

C-INSIDE THE TOMB AGAIN

Van Helsing has prepared everything for his dreadful task. The stake is sharpened with the end charred. He takes out from a surgical case a long scalpel, which he lays on the edge of the coffin. Then he says to Harker, "you must hold the stake in place just over the heart." Harker closes his eyes with horror, holds the stake in place, and Van Helsing picks up a great stone lying near, using it as a hammer to drive the stake thru Lucy's heart. As he raises the stone

    CUT TO:

C-22    SEWARD AND GODALMING-OUTSIDE

It is growing light. They listen and suddenly there is a wild agonizing wail from the inside of the tomb. Godalming attempts to enter the gate but is held back by Seward, and then covers his face with his hands in horror.

Van Helsing and Harker come out of the tomb, closing the door and locking it.

Van Helsing sees Godalming in suffering, and says: "that wild cry was not the cry of Lucy, but of the evil spirit which infested her body. Lucy is no longer undead. She is now at peace and her soul is saved. If you could see her face, you would believe me."

"Now for Carfax Abbey. The sun has risen and with luck, we shall find the monster sleeping in one of the coffins

    (CONTINUED)

C-22 (CONTINUED)

    where he must rest by day. We shall put this - (holding up the second stake) thru his heart and so destroy him and save our lovely Mina."

    The move toward the ruined Abbey, which is on the other side of the graveyard.

> N.B. If they still have the child, it could be sent to the gardener's cottage with Seward.

C-23 THE IRON-STUDDED DOOR OF THE ABBEY.

    With some difficulty they batter down the door and find themselves in a long corridor, thru which we have already seen Dracula disappear at the close of the second sequence.

    They come, by the light of the torches, to a stairway which leads apparently into the bowels of the earth. They descend this, the camera accompanying them, down - down - down, until they come to a great vaulted chamber, like that which Harker has already seen in the Castle Dracula.

> N.B. Weird sounds and what-not can accompany this descent.

    On the floor of the vaulted rooms are four coffin-like boxes. The place is filled with bats and in the back, at bay, glitter the red eyes of enumerable rats.

    Van Helsing, holding the Host before him and murmuring in Latin, advances into the unholy place. Harker exclaims, "there is no doubt, these are the same boxes I saw leaving Castle Dracula, but there were five of them."

    Van Helsing, bids them tear open the boxes. In one of them must be the undead body of Dracula, himself. The rats advance toward them as they begin work. Van Helsing , with the Host before him, drives

(CONTINUED)

C-23　(CONTINUED)

    them back. He says he will keep them at bay while the others perform the work. One by one they rip open the boxes. All are filled with earth, but none contain the form of Dracula. In dismay, Van Helsing exclaims, "he has escaped and hidden the fifth box else-where as a refuge. Unless we find it he has escaped and Mina is doomed. He has already put his stamp upon her. Unless we destroy him, he will claim her."

    Harker, in despair, cries, "What must we do? What can we do?" To which Van Helsing exclaims, "Only God, or a miracle can help us now. We must go at once to Mina."

C-24　MINA'S BEDROOM AGAIN

    The burly keeper and Mrs. Triplett have both fallen asleep in grotesque attitudes. On the bed, Mina, half unconscious, is moaning incoherently. The door opens gently and Harker and Van Helsing enter the room. Harker bends over her and is about to take her hand when Van Helsing says, in a hoarse whisper, wait... listen!"

    From the mutterings of Mina a few words become distinct. She murmurs. "Oh Master, don't leave me. Do not put the water between us. Do not go away".

    Van Helsing, in a fierce, excited whisper says, "Wait! Perhaps we have found a way to capture and destroy him. Perhaps God has delivered him into our hands."

    Bending over Mina, Van Helsing begins to stroke her forehead and to question her. In a low voice he says, "what do you see?" And in a hypnotic trance, Mina describes a ship with the name "Black Eagle" lying against the wharf, which they recognize from her description as the "Chelsea Pier".

    The ship is weighing anchor just as a coffin-like box is borne on board.

(CONTINUED)

C-24  (CONTINUED)

> Suddenly Mina wakens and recognizes John and Van Helsing. John attempts to embrace her. Again she cries out, "do not touch me, I am unclean". Van Helsing, straightening up, says, "we must act at once. Dracula is in that box. He is escaping and we must pursue him. He cannot escape so long as he is on a ship. A vampire cannot cross open water. Our chance of capturing him is when he lands between sunrise and sunset."
>
> In excitement Van Helsing shakes the keeper awake and orders him to bring a newspaper with the shipping new at once. The keeper obeys and steps out on the errand.
>
> John Harker, charges also with excitement, calls Seward and Godalming and excitedly breaks the news to them. They all plan to depart at once in pursuit. They set about preparing to go. Mina, rising in the bed insists that she accompany them and Van Helsing agrees with her. It is the only way to protect her in case Dracula has played them a trick of some kind. She must never be out of their sight.
>
> The keeper returns with the paper. Harker turns frantically to the ship news and finds that the "Black Eagle" has sailed at daybreak for Costanza, at which he cries, :he is fleeing to Castle Dracula." Van Helsing says, "if he gets there before us, everything is lost. He can hide himself away and sleep a hundred years, until we are all dead. We must catch him while he is still chained to that box of earth.

END OF SEQUENCE "C"

## SEQUENCE "D"

Sequence four is the race between the gypsies who are transporting the fifth box of earth, containing Dracula and the party consisting of Harker, Mina, Van Helsing, Godalming and Seward.

It is a race against time to capture the body of Dracula and put a stake thru his heart before sundown, when he can escape from the box and find refuge in his castle.

It is essentially a chance with very little dialogue and a great deal of action, ending in a fight with the gypsies just as they reach the door of the castle. When the box is captured it is opened and Dracula is found inside.
A stake is driven thru his heart, the body crumbles into dust and Mina is saved, and for the first time is taken in Harker's arms with safety.


N.B. It is well to note that an added suspense is given to the chase by the fact that each hour counts in saving Mina, who, as each hour progresses, drawn a little nearer toward her complete transformation into a vampire.

"DRACULA"

by

Louis Bromfield and Dudley Murphy

-------------------------------------------------------------------------
- - -

SEQUENCE "A"


FADE IN TO:

A-1   EXT CHURCHYARD FULL SHOT
      NIGHT MOONLIGHT

      This is an atmospheric shot with
      a suggestion of ground mist
      and the eerie moonlight throws
      long grotesque shadows from
      dimly perceptible tomb-
      stones.

      THE CAMERA IS MOVING SLOWLY
      THRU the churchyard as we
      are moving in.

      After we have fully faded in
      we hear the long howl of a
      wolf. THE CAMERA MOVES SLOWLY
      thru the churchyard towards
      a vault. As we approach the
      vault its door wings slowly
      open. Back of the vault can
      be seen other tombstones.
      The movement of the door is
      accompanied by two or three
      bats which fly slowly out
      into the haze as we DISSOLVE TO:


A-2   INT. HUNGARIAN PEASANT BEDROOM
      MEDIUM CLOSE SHOT DAY

      On a native bed lies a
      beautiful blonde baby girl
      with curly hair and six
      years old. The anxious mother
      and father stand in back of the bed
      awaiting the diagnoses of the doctor
      who is bending over the child's
      throat. The soft morning
      light filters thru a window
      in the background. The doctor
      slowly straightens up and
      gravely turns to the parents.                    (CONTINUED)

A-2   (CONTINUED)

          MOTHER      (she speaks in
                           Hungarian with a
                           pleading gesture, look-
                           -ing from the girl to
                           the doctor)

Is she better?

          DOCTOR      (shaking his head)

No! It's - baffling - - -
this loss of blood.

DISSOLVE TO:


A-3   EXT. NIGHT MISTY

Scene of a larger and more modern churchyard.

Across the scene comes the lonely howl of a wolf and a suggestion of bats flying across the scene. LAP DISSOLVE INTO:


A-4   INT. FRENCH MAIN OPERATING ROOM OF A MODERN PARIS HOSPITAL  FULL SHOT

Thru the glass skylight the room is brilliantly illuminated and we see a gallery of students behind a glass partition, watching the operating table, which is in the center. Around the operating table are two doctors, who are bending over the shrouded figure of a young girl patient. There are several nurses.

The whole atmosphere of the scene is modern and white. The CAMERA MOVES QUICKLY DOWN to a closeup of the group at the table. The Senior Doctor straightens up after his examination of the neck of the patient and baffled turns to the other doctor.

                                              (CONTINUED)

A-4    (CONTINUED)

                        DOCTOR        (In French
                                      (He shakes his head)
                                      It's baffling - this loss
                                      of blood.......

DISSOLVE TO:


A-5    EXT. NIGHT FULL SHOT
       LARGE ENGLISH CHURCHYARD

       There is the same suggestion
       of mist and in the sound
       track we hear again, the
       long howl of a wolf and
       a suggestion of bats flying
       across the scene.  LAP DISSOLVE
       TO:


A-6    INT. FULL SHOT WELL
       APPOINTED BEDROOM ENGLISH
       PEER HOME

       This is a large room and
       around the bed are grouped two
       doctors and two English trained
       nurses.  In the foreground, in a
       big chair, sits an aristocratic-
       looking woman of about 50 years,
       leaning with one hand on a
       walking stick and bending forward
       intently watching the doctor,
       who is bending over the patient.

       The patient is a beautiful young
       girl of seventeen or eighteen.
       The doctor is examining her neck.
       He straightens up, shakes his head
       and says:

                        DOCTOR

                                      It's baffling - the loss
                                      of blood...

                        MOTHER

                                      If it's not anemia, what is
                                      it, Doctor?

                        DOCTOR

                                      I don't know - none of us
                                      know.  There have been
                                      several cases reported lately.
                                      One is Paris last week.
                                             (CONTINUED)

69

A-6     (CONTINUED)

>                    The patient had three
>                    blood transfusions, but
>                    she died.

He pauses - looks down
at neck, taking magni-
fying glass from nurse, and
bending over patient looks
through glass.


A-7     CLOSEUP

Patient's neck, spots seen
through glass.

Over this scene we hear
the doctor's voice:

>               DOCTOR'S VOICE
>
>                    And in each case, these
>                    same two marks were
>                    found on the neck of the victim.


FADE OUT

SEQUENCE "B"

FADE IN:

B-1　　INT. PRIVATE LABORATORY
　　　 OF DR. VAN HELSING. BIG
　　　 CLOSEUP

Dr. Van Helsing's eyes are
seen thru heavy lenses,
which magnify his eyes so
that they fill the screen.
The eyes are staring directly
at an object beyond the
camera.

In the sound track we hear
the dripping of water, drip,
drip, drip, and the suggestion
of wind thru the trees.

We continue this scene with the
eyes staring fixedly ahead until
the effect gets ahold of us.
We then truck back very slowly
until we see the head and
shoulders of Dr. Van Helsing.
His eyes keep staring in the
same direction.
THE CAMERA TRUCKS BACK TO


B-2　　MED. SHOT

On the white glass table before
Van Helsing a microscope and
beside it a test tube half
filled with blood in a rack over
an alcohol lamp. Near Van Helsing
at the table is his assistant who is reading an enormous
book which lies on the table before him. Also at the table,
backs to camera and opposite
Van Helsing, sit three doctors.
They are the English doctor we
have seen in Sequence A, the
French Doctor and a little hunchback Austrian. Their attention
is concentrated on Dr. Van Helsing.
Van Helsing, with a pair of wire
tweezers, lifts the test tube and
tilting it carefully adds a
chemical which changes the color
in the tube with a sudden hissing
sound. He points dramatically
to his assistant, instructing him
to read. As the assistant starts
to read, in Latin, we CUT TO

B-3　　CLOSEUP OF A LARGE, OF FIFTEENTH-
　　　 CENTURY BOOK
It is printed in block Gothic type
and written in Latin which we do
not translate. The bony finger of
the assistant traces the words as
he reads.　 CUT TO:

B-4    CLOSEUP VAN HELSING

As he pours a single
drop of blood on a
glass slide. Over
this he places a tiny                We hear the voice of the
square of glass, and                 assistant reading in Latin
thrusts the whole under              from the book.
the microscope.

CUT TO:


B-5    MED. SHOT OF GROUP

They are all concen-
trating on Dr. Van Hel-
sing as he bends forward
and peers through the
microscope. He studies
it and slowly an expression
of horror comes over his
face. The doctors bend
closer, watching him in-
tently. He straightens
up and looks at them.

                          DOCTOR VAN HELSING
                              Gentlemen, our theory is con-
                              firmed. (Pause) We are dealing
                              with the undead.

The look at him, horrified,
in their realization. There
is an intake of breath.
The Austrian almost under
his breath -

                          AUSTRIAN
                              Nosferatu!

Van Helsing nods slowly.

                          VAN HELSING
                              Yes, the Vampire, the undead,
                              and earthbound creature that
                              leaves its grave at night to
                              feed on the blood of the living.

There is a pause as the
realize the import of his
discovery.

                          ENGLISH DOCTOR
                              Dr. Van Helsing, which patient's
                              blood proved the theory?

                          VAN HELSING
                              Case Number Nine, Renfield, in-
                              sane patient, confined in the
                              sanitarium of Dr. Seward, Whitby,
                              Yorkshire, England.

FADE OUT

SEQUENCE "C"

FADE IN

C-1   EXT. SEWARD'S SANITARIUM
      LATE AFTERNOON  CLOSEUP

      On a gate over which is an
      iron scroll reading "John
      Seward, Esq. Sanitarium"

      The camera trucks through
      the gate and we see the
      facade of the sanitarium.
      As we do so, we hear a
      blood-curdling scream and
      the camera pans rapidly
      along the facade and trucks
      to a barred window on the
      second floor. Thru the
      window we see Renfield on
      his knees, pleading with
      Martin the Keeper.

      CUT INSIDE:

C-2   INT. RENFIELD'S ROOM
      MED. SHOT

      As Renfield pleads, Martin
      is wrenching a fat spider
      from his hand. In disgust
      he throws it to the floor
      stepping on it.

                    MARTIN
                I'll teach you to leave those
                spiders and flies alone.

      Renfield pleads.

                You are going to eat what the
                doctor tells you to - - we
                are going to cure you.

      As he turns in disgust he
      sees some sugar on the
      window sill and with a
      gesture he brushes it to
      the floor.

                    MARTIN
                I am sick of this mania you
                have of trapping flies with
                sugar.

      He turns to the door.
      Renfield pleads with him
      with no avail. Martin
      goes out, slamming the
      door which doesn't com-
      pletely close. Renfield
      goes to the window sill,
      and as he starts to brush
      up the sugar which is on
      the floor he sees through
      the window the scene which
      attracts his attention. As
      he stares fixedly,

      CUT TO:

C-3    EXT. GROUNDS OF SEWARD
       HOME. LONG SHOT

       We see thru the trees from
       Renfield's point of view,
       the garden wall. On the wall
       Mina Seward is seated and
       John Harker stands with his
       arms around her waist beside
       her. Beyond them can be
       seen Whitby Harbor and the
       North Sea stretching out
       to meet the horizon. The
       CAMERA MOVES RAPIDLY down
       to a SEMI CLOSEUP OF THEM.


C-4    SEMI CLOSEUP JOHN AND MINA

                        MINA
                  Four weeks is a long, long time
                  dear - I'll be lonely.

                        JOHN
                  I'll miss you too, darling.

                        MINA
                  Somehow - I wish you weren't
                  going.

                        JOHN    (smiling)
                  but why, dear?

                        MINA
                  The Carpathian mountains! It
                  sounds so wild and far away.

                        JOHN
                  Nothing can happen to me.

       OFF SCENE is heard
       the voice of Renfield.

                        RENFIELD'S VOICE    (excited)
                  Don't let him go, Miss Mina
                  Don't let him go.

       Mina and John turn and
       we CUT TO:


C-5    MED. SHOT PAST MINA AND
       JOHN, OF RENFIELD

       As he comes in, Mina
       speaks to Renfield.
       Her manner is one of calm
       as she has been living in
       the Sanitarium for some
       times and treats him as
       a harmless lunatic.

                        JOHN
                  What's that?

              Continued

C-5  CONTINUED

>                    MINA    (jumping down from the wall,
>                             goes up to Renfield and pats
>                             him on the arm)
>
>                    RENFIELD
>                        Don't let him go, Miss Mina.
>                        Don't let him go to Transyvania.

CUT TO:

C-6  CLOSEUP OF JOHN

He reacts in astonishment.

>                    JOHN
>                        Why don't you want me to go to
>                        Transylvania?

CUT TO:

C-7  CLOSEUP OF RENFIELD

>                    RENFIELD    (intently)
>                        Don't ask me! Don't ask me!

CUT TO:

C-8  FULL SHOT OF HOUSE

On the portico stands Lucy and her uncle, Dr. Seward. The cart drives up in front of the house.

Thru the open door runs Martin, the Keeper. He is a blustering, burly character, like Wallace Beery. He blusters thru the door and appears very excited. He stops as he sees Dr. Seward.

>                    MARTIN    (to Dr. Seward)
>                        Beg pardon, Sir. But he's es-
>                        caped again.
>
>                    DR. SEWARD    (smiling tolerantly)
>                        Who's escaped, Martin?
>
>                    MARTIN    (exasperated almost beyond
>                               words)
>                        That spider eater - that fly
>                        eater - that bloke that's always
>                        craving life to eat. I'm losing
>                        weight keeping track of him.
>                        Heaven help me if he starts
>                        climbing trees after birds.

Contiinued

C-8        CONTINUED

                              DR. SEWARD    (smiles, looking off)
                                   There he is, Martin, with Miss
                                   Mina.

Martin goes off in
a blustering way as
if he was going to
kill him.

                              Dr. SEWARD    (calling after him)
                                   Be gentle with him, Martin.

Lucy, who has been
listening to all this,
looks seriously toward
Renfield. She turns to
her uncle and speaks
to him.

                              LUCY
                                   Uncle John, what would happen
                                   if you gave Renfield what he
                                   wants?

                              DR. SEWARD
                                   Why Lucy, why do you ask that?

     CUT TO:

C-9     MED, CLOSEUP OF
        DR. SEWARD

He is watching Lucy
closely as she answers
him.

                              LUCY    (slowly)
                                   I don't know (a pause)...I
                                   really don't know.

Lucy is looking off
toward the wall. Dr.
Seward follows her gaze.

     CUT TO:

C-10    MED. SHOT EXT GARDEN WALL

Martin has Renfield by the
arm.

                              MARTIN
                                   Come along, Renfield - come
                                   along. Tell them goodbye.

Renfield ignores Martin
and pleads with Mina

                              RENFIELD
                                   Don't let him go - don't let him
                                   go. I know - I know - I've been
                                   to Transylvania.
                              MARTIN    (whispering to him)
                                   Come - come, Renfield, I'll give

          continued

C-10  CONTINUED

                MARTIN
          you a lump of sugar so you can
          catch more files.

Renfield turns. His eyes are wild. Martin leads him out of scene.

Mina and John look after Renfield, sympathetically.

                JOHN       (turning to Mina
          He gets no better

                MINA       (shaking her head)

          No - worse. It's life - always
          life - - spiders - flies - -
          anything - - anything.
               (shudders)

As she shudders we hear Dr. Seward's voice.

                DR. SEWARDS'S VOICE    (calling)
          John, John, you'll miss your
          train.

As John looks at his watch, Mina looks off, calling.

                MINA
          All right, father - we're coming.

This snaps them out of their sympathetic attitude towards Renfield, John puts his arm around Mina and with ad lib conversation they exit.

CUT TO:


C-11  FULL SHOT FRONT OF HOUSE

The coachman has finished putting John's bags in the cart. Dr. Seward and Lucy go down to the cart as John and Mina hurriedly enter.

John shakes hands with Dr. Seward and kisses Lucy on the forehead, he then turns and helps Mina into the cart, climbing in himself, after her. The cart starts down the driveway. Dr. Seward glances at his watch and seeing that it is late, calls after the coachman.

                Continued

C-11    CONTINUED

> DR. SEWARD
> Peterson, you have to furry.
> Don't let Mr. Harker miss his
> train.

As the cart winds
down the driveway,
we CUT TO:

C-12    LONG SHOT OF DRIVEWAY
        WITH GATE IN FOREGROUND

We see the cart winding
down thru the beautiful
trees. The coachman
cracks his whip. Suddenly
the peacefulness of the
scene is broken by Renfield's
unearthly scream, as he comes
from behind some trees into
the middle of the gateway.

> RENFIELD (frantically)
> Don't let him go - don't let him
> go!

CUT TO:

C-13    EXT. ROAD  LONG SHOT

Of cart going down the
road. Mina and John are
facing us with their
backs to the horse. They
are paying no attention
to Renfield. John has his
arm around Mina, and we
see him bending close to
her, as the cart jogs off.

CUT TO:

C-14    MED. SHOT OF RENFIELD

He is standing in the
gateway frantically
calling after them.

> RENFIELD
> For Heaven's sake, Miss Mina,
> don't let him go - don't let him
> go -

In the background, Martin,
the keeper, can be seen
lumbering towards Renfield
as we

FADE OUT.

SEQUENCE "D"

D-1  FADE IN EXTERIOR TRANSYL-
     VANIA MOUNTAIN PASS. LONG SHOT

   On a narrow mountain gorge in
   the wildest part of Transylvania.
   In the background the sun is just
   setting. Thru the gorge and
   approaching the camera, comes a
   mountain coach, drawn by four
   horses at top speed.
   CUT TO:

D-2  SEMI-CLOSE SHOT

   Taken from in front of the
   coach toward the driver as
   he is encouraging the horses
   on.
   DISSOLVE TO:

D-3  INTERIOR COACH. MED. SHOT

   There are two long seats
   running lengthwise in the
   coach. The passengers are
   a mannish-looking Englishwoman in tweeds. Her secretary, a little mouse-
   like woman, with thick
   glasses. Two natives of
   Transylvania, husband and
   wife who speak broken English and their little four
   year old girl, and John
   Harker.
   The people are being jostled
   about uncomfortably as the
   coach charges at break-neck
   speed over the bad road.
   The Englishwoman, however,
   has her feet braced against
   the seat opposite her and is
   stoic in her lack of concern.
   Her secretary is reading from
   a Beadeker.

                    SECRETARY
               "Approaching Bistritz, the road
               leads through the heart of the
               Carpathians, one of the wildest
               and least know-known parts of Europe."

   The coach lurches and she
   is shot across the aisle,
   into Harker's lap. She re-
   covers her composure and with
   the aid of Harker gets seated
   as the Englishwoman who has
   paid no attention to Sara,
   the secretary's discomposure

                    ENGLISHWOMAN
               Where were we, Sara
                    SARA
               "The wildest and least-known
               parts of Europe."

        CONTINUED

                                79

D-3     CONTINUED

                    ENGLISHWOMAN
                        Continue, Sara.

                    SARA
                        "Among its rugged peaks are
                        found crumbling castles of a
                        bygone age."

Again the coach lurches
and she is thrown again
at Harker who is seated
opposite her. John
assists her, smiling,
and leans forward to
speak to driver who can
be seen through a square
window in the front of
the coach.

                    HARKER
                        A bit slower.

The native husband grabs
Harker's arm and pulls
him back -

                    NATIVE
                        No, no, - look!

They all look from the
window and we see

CUT TO:


D-4     LONG SHOT

Taken through window, of
a beautiful sunset against
the jagged peaks of the
mountains.
CUT BACK TO:

D-5     INTERIOR COACH. MED. SHOT

As John and passengers look
back from window. John is
looking quizzically at the
native as -

                    ENGLISHWOMAN
                        What are they looking at, Sara?

                    SARA
                        A sunset

                    ENGLISHWOMAN
                        Get the kodak. Have the driver
                        stop.

Sara reaches for the
kodak and putting her
hand through the window
in the front of the coach
pulls the

        (continued)

D-5   CONTINUED

driver's coat-tails,
telling him to stop
but the native peasant
excitedly stops her -

> NATIVE
> No, no, he must not stop. We
> must reach the Inn by sundown.

The Englishwoman turns
to the Hungarian.

> ENGLISHWOMAN (Coldly)
> And why!

The native leans forward
superstitiously and in a
sort of hoarse whisper as
if he was almost afraid to
speak -

> NATIVE
> It is St. George's Eve - the
> night the evil spirits roam.

Sara reacts. Her eyes roll
in terror. The Englishwoman
is intolerant and with her
nose in the air sniffs and
looks at Harker as if to say,
:What can you expect from
these stupid peasants?"
The peasant is annoyed by her
attitude and leans forward -

> NATIVE
> If you lived in these parts,
> you would not sneer. It is a
> night, madame, when doors are
> barred and prayers are offered
> to the Virgin.

As he is speaking,
DISSOLVE TO:

D-6   INT. NATIVE HUT. FULL SHOT

At the window an old man is
hanging some herbs against
the glass. He is muttering
to himself in Hungarian, and
crosses himself. He goes
to the door and places a little
lighted oil lamp at the foot
of an Ikon which is fastened
over the door. And old woman
is seated in the foreground,
telling her rosary in Hungarian.
This continued prayer of hers
is heard throughout the entire
scene                           Monotonous, Intense prayer.
Over a peasant cradle a young
girl is bending. In the
cradle is a baby. The girl
takes the baby in her arms
sees that it is all right,
                                Continued

D-6    CONTINUED

Puts a little
crucifix around its neck
and lays it gently back
in the cradle.
The white-haired old man
with a piece of chalk draws
a Maltese Cross on the door.

DISSOLVE TO:


D-7    EXT. COURTYARD OF INN. FULL
       SHOT. DUSK

In the foreground are two big
gates through which we see the
Inn, a ramshackled, bedraggled
building with thatched and
jutting roof. All the angles
and shadows are weird and
sinister. In front of it hangs
a sign with a wolf's head painted
on it, and a small fir tree
which is hung upsidedown.

In back of the Inn the last rays
of the sun can be seen disappear-
ing over the distant mountain
peaks. Thru open gates we hear
the sound of horses' hoofs in
the distance. The door of the Inn
opens. The Proprietor comes out,
looks toward the camera, turns
back and calls someone in Hungarian. The Proprietor's wife and
porter come out excited. As they
do so the stage coach dashes in
the gates. It pulls up in front
of the Inn and stops. As the porter
runs forward to close the gates, we
DISSOLVE TO:


B-8    CLOSER SHOT OF COACH NEAR TAVERN DOOR

The driver hurriedly gets down
from seat, starts to unhitch
the horses. Peasants climb down
from the coach, greet the proprietor and wife and exit into
Inn.

Englishwoman and secretary also exit
into Inn. John Harker, as he gets
out of stage, speaks to the Proprietor:

                    JOHN HARKER
                Will I have time for tea before
                the coach leaves?

The Proprietor who is
standing there nervous, tells
the driver in Hungarian to hurry
up get inside.
                            CONTINUED)

D-8    CONTINUED

Turns back to John

          PROPRIETOR
             The coach goes no farther to-
             night.

He exits toward Inn.
John starts after him
and says -

          JOHN HARKER
             I say - wait!

They exit thru door

CUT TO:

D-9    INT. TAPROOM OF INN.
       MED. SHOT

The taproom of the inn is
'a low, sinister room with
enormous beams. A fire is
burning in one corner and
the shutters and door are
all marked with Maltese
crosses made in chalk. In
the background are a half
dozen natives of the most
wild and savage appearance,
sitting at tables. At one
end of the room is a stairway leading to a balcony
from which a door leads the bed-
rooms.

The proprietor enters,
followed by John

          JOHN HARKER
             Do I understand you to say this
             coach does not go on tonight?

          PROPRIETOR
             It's St. George's Eve.

          ENGLISHWOMAN
             I know. I heard all about St.
             George's Eve - the haunted castle -
             evil spirits.

          PROPRIETOR
             I have seen their victims.

the wife and Proprietor
are standing near and cross
themselves.

          HARKER
             But see here - I must reach Borgo
             Pass by midnight. There's a
             carriage to meet me there.

CUT TO:

D-10    CLOSEUP PROPRIETOR

                        PROPRIETOR    (in a hoarse whisper)
                            Whose carriage?

        CUT TO:

D-11    CLOSE-UP JOHN HARKER

                        JOHN HARKER
                            Count Dracula's!

        (We hear an intake of breath from the
         people in the Inn. Then a moment of
         deathly silence, followed by a sudden
         uncanny scream) and we

        CUT TO:

D-12    CLOSEUP OF PROPRIETOR'S
        WIFE

        as she is clutching the
        crucifix. She is staring
        at John Harker. She rushes
        out of scene.

        CUT TO:

D-13    MED. SHOT WHERE HARKER IS
        STANDING

        She rushes in a falls on
        her knees in front of him
        and holds the crucifix up to
        his face. Harker stares at
        it. The Proprietor's voice
        comes across the scene and
        says -
                        PROPRIETOR'S VOICE  (in a hoarse whis
                            Dracula!          per)

        CUT TO:

D-14    GLASS SHOT OF WEIRD, RUINED
        CASTLE

        On a jagged mountain top.

        DISSOLVE TO:

D-15    INT. CRYPT IN THE BOWELS
        OF CASTLE DRACULA. FULL SHOT

        As we are dissolving, the
        camera in no motion, approaching
        some coffin-like boxes which
        lie in the crypt. Through a
        lattice-like, Gothic window
        the last rays of the sun can
        be seen, throwing a fantastic
        shadow on the wall. There is
        a sinister atmosphere in this

                            continued

                                84

D-15   CONTINUED

    crypt, a suggestion of movement of weird animals on the floor. The camera moves slowly up to the corner of one of the boxes and as it does so, we see the fingers of one of Dracula's hands coming under the lid of the box. As the hand emerges, we pan the camera to the light effect on the wall, The sun goes down and as the light effect disappears, we pan back, and Dracula is discovered with his back to camera, bending over and closing the box. He straightens up and slowly glides toward camera. We keep him in the lens until his eyes entirely fill the screen as he approaches. He walks right into the camera, fading the picture out.

    We hear the long howl of a wolf which carries over into the next scene.

CUT TO:

D-16   INT. OF TAPROOM OF INN.
      MED. SHOT

    John has money and is arguing with the proprietor and driver about the price of the coach. As the wolf's cry dies out, the natives cross themselves.

                  HARKER
          I will give you twenty pounds sterling, and drive the coach myself. I will return it in the morning.

D-17   HARKER, PROPRIETOR, DRIVER
      FULL SHOT

    The three are in the foreground. In the background are the terror-stricken faces of the peasants, listening and watching. The Driver accepts John's proposition. The peasants are horrified as they realize John is about to leave. As the bargain is closed, John looks towards his bags.

                  Continued

D-17    CONTINUED

                         HARKER
                    Have the boy put my bags in the
                    coach.

No one will budge and
John, exasperated, grabs
his handbag and portfolio
and starts toward the
door, muttering in dis-
gust. The proprietor
moves toward him and stops
him at door.

CUT TO:

D-18    SEMI-CLOSE OF DOOR

As Proprietor points his
finger at John.

                         PROPRIETOR
                    Do you know where you are going
                    and what you are going to do?

John has lost patience
by this time.
                         HARKER
                    Yes, I know - I know

The proprietor sees it
is hopeless and moves
away. John turns to
leave.

CUT TO:

D-19    PROPRIETOR. MED. CLOSE SHOT

His wife runs up to him and
talks to him hurriedly in
Hungarian, holding the crucifix. The Proprietor shakes
his head in disgust and the
woman turns toward John, calling to him and runs out.

CUT TO:

D-20    HARKER AT THE DOOR
        MED. CLOSE SHOT

He turns as the proprietor's
wife runs in. She puts the
crucifix over John's head.

                         PROPRIETOR'S WIFE
                    Wear it for your mother's sake, -
                    wear it - - it will protect you.

John, to please her,
accepts the gesture and
opens the door -

                         CONTINUED

D-20   CONTINUED

         HARKER
          All right - - all right.

Proprietor comes in, unbolts the door and holds it ajar just a crack. John takes his bags and exits. As he does so, we hear the howl of a wolf.

CUT TO:

D-21   CORNER OF ROOM. MED SHOT

As the natives hear the howl of the wolf cross themselves. The Englishwoman is disgusted and annoyed by the superstition of the natives and in disgust motions to Sara to place the gold stick seat which we have planted before, for her to sit on. Sara, however, is staring towards the door as she is holding the stick, scared by the wolf's cry, and confusedly and with her mind of the wolf, she places the stick with the seat down and the point up. (Note: This action is taking place in the foreground of the shot).

CUT TO:

D-22   DOOR AS JOHN EXITS. MED. CLOSE SHOT

Proprietor slams door and bolts it.

CUT TO:

D-23   SARA. MED CLOSE SHOT

As she places stick for Englishwoman, point up. Englishwoman sits down on it. The point sticks her, and with a scream she takes it big. The natives cross themselves

         Over this scene, we hear
         the sound of prancing
         of horses' hoofs.

CUT TO:

D-24   EXT. COURTYARD
       FULL SHOT

       As Harker, having
       climbed to the seat of
       the coach is starting
       the horses out onto the
       road. As the coach
       moves out onto the road,
       we see the curtains
       pulled back from one of
       the windows of the Inn
       and the Proprietor wife's
       eyes in the window.


D-25   THE WINDOW, CLOSE SHOT

       As we see through it, the
       Proprietor's wife's face        Over this we hear the crack of a
       pressed against the pane.       whip and the carriage wheels
       She crosses herself and         moving out down the road. As
       raises her hands in prayer.     they die out, we hear the long
                                       howl of a wolf.

       From the woman's terror-
       stricken face against the
       pane, we DISSOLVE TO


D-26   EXT TRANSYLVANIA MOUNTAINS
       BORGO PASS AT CROSS-ROADS
       FULL SHOT

       Moonlit, cloudy sky.
       Here, on a pile of rocks, is
       a primitive cross marking a
       grave. Up the road, beyond
       the cross comes the coach
       driven by Harker. It halts
       at the cross and Harker climbs
       down, taking the bridle of the
       horses in his hand. With the
       other hand he takes out his
       watch and looks at the
       time.
       INSERT OF WATCH
       It is twelve o'clock.

       CUT TO:


D-27   EXT. TRANSYLVANIAN MTS.
       MED. SHOT AT CROSSROADS

       As Harker surveys the barren
       countryside. He takes out
       his two bags and as he starts
       to attach the horses to a
       dad tree by the side of the
       road, a nearby wolf howls.      Howl of wolf ... nearby.

D-28    EXT. TRANSYLVANIA MTS.
        CLOSEUP OF HORSES

    As they rear, and with a
    terrific whine, gallop
    down the road, throwing        Horses whine
    Harker to one side as they    Gallop of hoofs, etc.
    go.


D-29    EXT. TRANSYLVANIA MTS.
        FULL SHOT AT CROSSROADS

    As the horses' hoofs die
    out, there is a moment of
    deathly silence, then as       Horses' hoofs....distant.
    if from a wide circle around
    him, comes the howling of     Encircling howling of
    wolves.                                wolves.

    A mist rises and obliterates
    the moon and accompanying
    the mist comes the sound of
    horses' hoofs.               Approaching horses' hoofs.

    Harker, for a moment, thinks
    that the horses are returning,
    but then notices that this
    new sound of hoofs is from
    a different direction and
    then, as if dissolving out
    of a mist, there appears a
    fantastic cabriolet drawn
    by two black horses, with a
    driver on the box. It comes
    up a wild gallop, halting
    before Harker, who looks up
    at the Driver.


D-30    EXT. TRANSYLVANIAN MTS.
        CLOSEUP HARKER AT CROSSROADS

    His reaction as he looks up
    at the Driver. We CUT TO
    what he sees:


D-31    SEMI CLOSE SHOT  LOOKING UP
        FROM HARKER's POINT OF VIEW
        TOWARD DRIVER.

    He is wrapped in a great coat
    with a black hat pulled down over
    his eyes. The collar of the coat
    is turned up so that all that is
    visible are two burning eyes.

D-32    CROSSROADS. MED. SHOT

As the Driver opens the
door and motions Harker
in. Harker, hypnotized
for the moment by the
eyes, stares at him, then
handing his bags up to the
driver, he gets in.


D-33    EXT. TRANSYLVANIA MTS.
FULL SHOT AT CROSSROADS

As the coach starts to move,
the mist which surrounded it
on its arrival, gathers and
as we hear the horses' hoofs
start up in a gallop
the mist obliterates the dis-
appearing coach and in CLOUDS
forms BEFORE THE CAMERA.
Thru these clouds which we
continue to photograph can
be heard the clatter of horses          Horses' hoofs'
hoofs. This continues for                starting up.
several seconds and then as the
mist clears, we see:                     Horses hoof's continued


D-34    INT OF COACH. MED. SHOT

We hear the continuation of
the horses' hoofs, galloping            Speeding Hoofs
apparently at xxxxxxxxx                      (continued)
breakneck speed.

Harker is being jostled about
so terrifically that he leans
forward and looks out of the
window to speak to the driver.

CUT TO:


D-35    EXT. ANGLE SHOT DRIVER'S
SEAT. FROM HARKER'S VIEWPOINT

There is still a slight mist
which seems to cling to it
and we see distinctly that the
Driver is missing...but above
the horses' heads flies a great
bat.

D-36   CLOSEUP OF HARKER

   His head sticking out
   of the window of carriage.
   He is mystified by what
   he has seen.
   DISSOLVE TO:


D-37   EXT. MINIATURE SHOT

   of a weird, fantastic
   castle on the mountain
   top, as up the winding
   road the carriage
   approaches.
   DISSOLVE TO:


D-38   REAL CASTLE. ANGLE SHOT

   With big, massive oak gates
   in the foreground, with the
   fantastic castle rising
   behind it.

   The coach comes past the
   camera as the horses' hoofs
   grow louder and as it
   approaches, the gates
   majestically swing open to
   admit the coach.

   Thru the gates we see the
   coach advancing to another
   great iron-studded door of
   the castle itself in the
   courtyard.


D-39   EXT. FRONT OF CASTLE COURT-
   YARD. MED.SHOT

   The carriage is before the
   door. Harker gets out in
   bewilderment. There is no
   driver and his bags are gone.
   As he stands there for a
   moment in the courtyard the
   inner door to the castle opens
   of its own accord. Harker
   enters.

   CUT TO:

D-40    INT. LONG TUNNEL-LIKE
        HALL  TRUCK SHOT

   The door closes behind
   Harker. Harker, as if
   drawn by some mysterious
   force, approaches. The
   camera slowly follows
   trucking back with him
   as he glances about in
   astonishment and slowly
   approaches. We now ..
   CUT TO:


D-41    TRUCK SHOT OF HALL

   From Harker's point of
   view. Camera slowly
   advances.

   The hall is a long tunnel-
   like vaulted room lighted
   by three or four large
   candles stuck in sconces
   along the wall. There are
   two or three suits of armor
   in bad state of repair and
   covered with blood stains.
   They are leaning back
   against the wall.

   The camera panning reveals
   these things in turn and
   while panning moves forward.
   Near a Gothic window in the
   upper part of the hallway
   some bats hang from some
   tapestry, and suddenly they
   flutter away.
   A curtain moves mysteriously.
   As the camera follows down the
   hall, it comes to a big door
   which opens of its own accord.
   The camera passes through
   and the door is heard to                Sound of door being
   close and bolt itself my-               closed and bolted.
   steriously.
   The camera comes to a great
   staircase which leads up
   and up and up into the upper
   part of the castle. As the
   camera rounds a turn in this
   staircase, we suddenly see a
   giant and dust-covered cobweb
   which is stretched completely
   across the hall as if spun by
   some gargantuan spider. In
   front of it stands Dracula.

   Dracula is a tall, thin man
   of distinguished appearance.
   His lips are pale but his large
   eyes burn with a weird glow
   and can be recognized at once

                                           Continued

D-41  CONTINUED

    as those of the coachman. He is dressed in a kind of black, officer's uniform, or full dress, with a ribbon on his shirt front. In manner her has a sinister distinction and is suave and polite in a cold blooded way.

D-42  HARKER. SEMI-CLOSE

    From Dracula's point of view as he stares in surprise at seeing someone for the first time.
    CUT TO:

D-43  SHOOTING UP STAIRWAY TAKING IN BOTH HARKER AND DRACULA. MED. SHOT

    Dracula bows -

        DRACULA
            I am Dracula. I bid you welcome.

    Harker is too surprised to speak and is inarticulate, and as he stares we hear the long howl of a wolf nearby, answered by another howl of a wolf in the distance. Harker is nervous
    CUT TO:

D-44  DRACULA. CLOSEUP

    As he speaks -

        DRACULA
        Listen them - the children of the night - what music they make!

    CUT BACK TO:

D-45  DRACULA AND HARKER MED. SHOT

        DRACULA
        It is late. My people are not available.

D-46  DRACULA. CLOSEUP

    As he continues with a gesture, motioning Harker to follow him.

        Continued

D-46   CONTINUED

>                    DRACULA
>           If you will please follow me.

He turns and starts
up the stairway toward
the cobweb. Camera
follows him as he
approaches cobweb.
As he comes up to it,
we CUT TO:


D-47   HARKER CLOSEUP

Preceded by camera taken
through cobweb. He
suddenly stops and stares
in astonishment.
CUT TO:


D-48   DRACULA AND HARKER. MED SHOT

As dracula continues up stairs
on the other side of cobweb.
Harker can hardly believe his
eyes, but as Dracula waits for
him to follow, Harker breaks
cobweb nervously and continues.
CUT TO:

D-49   A GIANT SPIDER, QUICK PAN SHOT

As spider is disturbed by
Harker and scurries up the
wall.
CUT TO:


D-50   DRACULA. SEMI-CLOSE SHOT

As he comes to head of staircase. He turns, looks back
at Harker.

>                    DRACULA
>           The walls of my castle are
>           broken and the shadows are many.
>           I am the last of my race.

   CUT TO:

D-51  UPPER HALLWAY.
      REVERSE ANGLE.
      MED. SHOT

   Through broken crevices
   of the wall moonlight
   filters. As Dracula
   finishes speaking, he
   crosses hall to a
   door, followed by Harker.
   As Dracula opens door and
   holds it for Harker,
   Camera moves up to them
   and shoots through door
   past them into a luxurious-
   ly appointed and comfortable
   bedroom. An open fire is
   burning in a big stone fireplace.
   John enters and the camera
   follows Dracula through, con-
   tinuing to shoot into the room.
   They stand backs to the camera.
   John reacts to the room's com-
   fort. Ad Dracula closes door,
   he turns to Harker and smiles.

                    DRACULA
               I did not expect you to feel
               at home among my dust and cob-
               webs.

   CUT TO:

D-52  INT. BEDROOM. REVERSE
      ANGLE. MED. SHOT

   John is relieved and as
   Dracula leaves door, he
   moves to a table which
   is laid for supper. There
   is a solid silver ser-
   vice and the whole atmosphere of the room is one of
   tremendous wealth.
   As Dracula indicates table -

                    DRACULA
               Come, your supper awaits you.

   john hesitates -

                    HARKER
               I am afraid I haven't much
               appetite, Sir

   Dracula takes a bottle
   of wine from the table
   and placing a seat for
   Harker insists on his
   sitting down. As he pours
   the wine he hands the glass
   to Harker.

                    DRACULA
               Well at least - a glass of wine
               to refresh you.

On August 26, 1930 Lon Chaney died. This is where the script being prepared for him stopped. During the confused weeks that followed Universal decided not to drop the project for they already had Chaney's director Tod Browning under contract.

Following are the titles for the 1931 silent version if Lugosi's Dracula

FINISHED NEGATIVE TITLES & INSERTS             PICTURE #109-2 BROWNING
                                                              (SILENT)

                         U N I V E R S A L
                              PART I
PART TITLE                  "D R A C U L A"

                     ———

           FADE IN - PICTORIAL ANIMATED MAIN TITLE

                      CARL   LAEMMLE

                       "D R A C U L A'

                           With

                        BELA LUGOSI

                 From the book by BRAM STOKER

                  A TOD BROWNING PRODUCTION

                 PRODUCED BY CARL LAEMMLE, JR.


            Copyright MCMXXXI by Universal Pictures Corp.

                    Carl Laemmle, President

                         DISSOLVES INTO:

                      ———

Associate Producer          E.M. Asher

Playscript                  Garrett Fort

Art Director                Charles D. Hall

              MPPDA

Titles                      Gardener Bradford

Cinematographer             Karl Freund

Supervising Film Editor     Maurice Pivar

               ...DISSOLVES INTO

                      ———

             DIRECTED BY TOD BROWNING

                     ...DISSOLVES TO

                      ———

## THE PLAYERS

```
Count Dracula............BELA LUGOSI
Mina         ...............HELEN CHANDLER
John Harker  ........... DAVID MANNERS
Renfield................. Dwight Frye
Van Helsing............. Edward Van Sloan
Dr. Seward  ............ Herbert Bunston
Lucy         .................Frances Dade
Maid         ................ Joan Standing
Martin       .............  Charles Gerrard
                    ...FADE OUT
```

S.T.

1 "- - approaching Bistritz, the road crosses the Carpathians mountains, one of the wildest parts of Central Europe."

2 "Tell the driver to slow up."

3 "No! No! We must reach the Inn before sundown! It is Walpurgis night - - a night of evil!"

4 "Don't take my luggage down - - I'm going on to Borgo Pass."

5 "The driver asks if you can't wait until morning. It is Walpurgis night - - he is afraid!"

6 "I'm sorry - - but at midnight I am to met the carriage of Count Dracula."

7 "You mustn't go! Dracula is one of the un-dead-- a vampire! On this night, he and his wives leave their coffins - - "

8 "Sometimes they take the form of bats - for wolves!"

9 "But this is all superstition —"

10 "The sun is setting! Soon Dracula and his wives will come out of their coffins to feast on the blood of the living."

S.T.

11   "But I must go - - it's important business."

12   "Wear this cross for your mother's sake —
     It will protect you."

13   "Is this the coach to Count Dracula?"

14   "I am Dracula!"

15   "For a moment, I thought I was in the
     wrong place!"

16   "The walls of my castle are broken but
     come - - I bid you welcome."

            U N I V E R S A L

               END OF PART
                   1
                DRACULA

            U N I V E R S A L

                  PART
                   2
                DRACULA

17   "The eternal struggle for life - - the
     spider spinning his web for the unwary
     fly!"

18   "The blood is the life, Mr. Renfield!"

19   "I ordered some food for you - - I thought
     you might be hungry."

20   "I thrust you have kept your coming here
     a secret."

21   "I have followed your instructions implicitly."

22   "And now, if you are not to fatigued, I
     would like to discuss the lease of Carfax
     Abbey,"

S.T.

23        "I trust I brought enough labels for you luggage."

24        "I am taking with me only three - - boxes."

25        "Tomorrow, I shall be elsewhere - - but we will meet after sundown."

26        "I hope you will find this bed comfortable."

27        "It's nothing serious - - just a cut from the paper clip."

28        "This is very old wine - - I hope you will like it."

29        "Oh, aren't you drinking?"

30        "I never drink - - wine."

31        "I have chartered a boat and we will leave for England tomorrow evening."

32        FADE IN
               Aboard the Vesta - - bound for England.

                               FADE OUT

33        "Master! The sun is down!"

34        "No! No! Spare the crew, or the ship will be wreaked!"

35        FADE IN PICTORIAL
               LONDON
                      word dissolves into scene

                           U N I V E R S A L

                               END OF PART 2

                                 DRACULA

UNIVERSAL

PART 3

DRACULA

———

S.T.

| | |
|---|---|
| 36 | "After you have delivered th emessage you will remember nothing I now say!" |
| 37 | "You are wanted on the telephone, Doctor Seward." |
| 38 | "Might I inquire if you are the Doctor Seward whose sanitarium is at Whitby?" |
| 39 | "I'm Count Dracula. I have leased Carfax Abbey which adjoins your grounds." |
| 40 | "May I present my daughter, Mina." |
| 41 | "Miss Lucy Weston and Mr. Harker." |
| 42 | "Count Dracula has just leased Carfax Abbey." |
| 43 | "Carfax Abbey reminds me of my own castle in Transylvania." |
| 44 | "The Abbey always reminds me of the toast - - " |
| 45 | " - - 'Lofty Timers - - the walls around are bare - -echoing out laughter as though the dead were there'." |
| 46 | "To die - - to be really dead - - that must be glorious!" |
| 47 | "There are far warse things awaiting man than death." |
| 49 | "The third death - - and in each case, the same two tiny marks appear on the throat." |
| 50 | "Miss Weston like the others died from an unnatural loss of blood." |

CHEM. FADE IN

INSERT #1
                   CLOSE UP OF NEWSPAPER INSERT
                        LATE LONDON EDITION
               MYSTERIOUS DEATH ATTRIBUTED
                    TO STRANGE MALADY
               MEDICAL PROFESSION BAFFLED.
                  Dr. Seward Consults Eminent Specialist,
                      Prof. Van Helsing
            Following a series of mysterious deaths in
            London and...etc

S.T.

50            "Doctor Seward, we are dealing with the
               undead - - the vampire."

51            "But Professor Van Helsing - - modern
               science doesn't admit of any such creature!"

52            "Yet this experiment proves Lucy to be the
               victim of one of the very creatures whose
               existence you deny."

53            "We must search for someone who believes
               he must have the blood of living things to
               sustain his own life - -"

54            "When we have found that person I will prove
               that the superstition of yesterday is the
               scientific reality of today!"

55            "Spiders now is it? Flies ain't good enough
               for you!"

56            "Flies? Poor puny things! Who wants to eat flies?"

57            "You do, you looney - -ever since we found you
               crazy on that bloomin' boat."

58            "Not while I can get nice fat spiders!"

59            "All right, come along now - - the doctor
               wants to see you."

60            "Your description of the man Renfield, who was
               taken off the Vesta, convinces me we are on the
               right track."

S.T.

61 "I'm professor Van Helsing -- I am here to help you, Renfield."

62 "Keep your filthy hands to yourself!"

63 "Doctor Seward! Send me away! My cries at night might disturb Miss Mina."

64 "They might give her bad dreams, Professor Van Helsing -- bad dreams."

U N I V E R S A L

END OF PART
3

DRACULA

U N I V E R S A L

PART 4

DRACULA

65 "What was the unearthly wail?"

66 "It sounded like a wolf."

67 " 'E thinks they're wolves! 'E thinks they're talking to him! 'E's crazy!"

68 "Mr. Renfield, we know how to make them stop!"

69 "You know too much to live, Van Helsing!"

70 "We won't get any more out of him tonight."

71 "On yer way, fly-eater!"

72 "I'm warning you! IF you don't send me away, you must answer for what will happen to Miss Mina!"

73 "What is that herb that excited him so?"

74 "Wolfbane! The natives of Central Europe wear it to protect themselves against vampires."

| | |
|---|---|
| S.T. | |
| 75 | "You say Renfield escapes from his cell at night. Have him closely watched -- see where he goes." |
| 76 | "No! No, Master! Not her -- not her!" |
| 77 | "Don't, Master! You took Lucy -- please don't harm Mina!" |
| 78 | FADE IN<br>　　　The following evening --<br><br>　　　　　　　　　　　FADE OUT |
| 79 | "I had a terrible dream last night --" |
| 80 | "-- I thought I heard an unearthly howling -- and then it seemed as though the room filled with mist." |
| 81 | "And then I saw two red eyes staring at me -- and a livid white face looking down out of the mist." |
| 82 | "It came closer and closer. I felt it's breath -- and then its lips --" |
| 83 | "Those lips you felt in the dream -- where did they touch you?" |
| 84 | "How long have you had those little marks on your throat?" |
| 85 | "I first noticed them this morning." |
| 86 | "What could have caused them?" |
| 87 | "I trust I do not intrude." |
| 88 | "On the contrary, you are most welcome." |
| 89 | "Pardon me! Count Dracula, meet Professor Van Helsing." |

| S.T. | |
|---|---|
| 90 | "Van Helsing! A most distinguished scientist, whose name we know, even in Transylvania." |
| 91 | "I had a frightful dream last night - - I can't get it out of my mind." |
| 92 | "I hope you haven't taken my stories too seriously." |
| 93 | "I endeavored to amuse your fiancee with some grim tales of my far off country." |
| 94 | "I can imagine." |
| 95 | "I think, Mina, that you had better retire." |
| 96 | "I am sorry that my visit was so ill-timed." |
| 97 | "On the contrary, you may be of very definite service." |

U N I V E R S A L

END OF PART
4

DRACULA

U N I V E R S A L

PART 5

DRACULA

| | |
|---|---|
| 98 | "A moment ago I stumbled upon an amazing phenomenon - - " |
| 99 | " - - something so incredible I distrust my own judgment." |
| 100 | "My humble apologies - - it was unavoidable." |

S.T.

101      "For one who has not lived even a single lifetime, you are a wise man, Van Helsing."

102      "What's that running across the lawn? It looks like a wolf!"

103      "Dracula is our vampire! He is responsible for Lucy's death -- for the marks on Mina's throat."

104      " I thought you suspected Renfield!"

105      "A vampire casts no reflection in the mirror! That proves that Dracula, not Renfield, is our man."

106      "Be guided by what he says -- it is your only hope!"

107      "Take Mina away before -- "

108      "No! No, Master! I didn't tell them anything! I'm loyal, Master -- I'm loyal!"

109      "What have you to do with Dracula?"

110      "I never heard the name before!"

111      "If you don't tell the truth you'll die in torment with innocent blood on your soul."

112      "No! No! God knows the powers of evil are too great for those with weak minds!"

113      "Miss Mina's lying out there -- on the lawn --"

114      "Try and tell me exactly what happened."

115      "I remember a dense red mist -- and two red eyes that drew me forward with a hypnotic power I could not resist -- "

116      "-- they drew me nearer -- and nearer --until I could see a face -- that same livid face that came to me in my dream."-

S.T.

117 "Miss Mina, I promise that from this moment, you will be released from this horror."

118 "I am afraid it is too late, Professor Van Helsing. Something tells me I am about to die."

119 "Darling, you're not going to die -- you're going to live!"

120 "It's all over, John -- all our love -- our life together --"

121 "Please explain to him -- I can't."

122 "Miss Mina, you must come in-door!"

123 "If Mina's in danger, I'm going to protect her!"

124 "Mina's going with me to London! If you can't save her, I will!"

125 "I must be master here! This room will be guarded with wolfbane -- to prevent Dracula's return."

126 "Say what you like -- Mina's going with me!"

127 "Miss Mina is to wear this wreath of wolfbane around her neck. See that she does not remove it in her sleep.

128 "But you don't understand, Mr. Harker! The vampire appears only at night! During the day, it must rest on the earth in which it was buried."

129 "But that's ridiculous! Dracula would have to return every night to Transylvania!"

130 "He must have brought boxes of his native soil to rest in by day - we must find the, and drive a stake through his heart."

S.T.

131  "Gentlemen!"

132  "Isn't this a strange conversation for men who are supposedly sane?"

133  "Renfield! I shall have to put you in a straight-jacket!"

134  "The doctor's pet looney is loose again."

UNIVERSAL

END OF PART
5

DRACULA

UNIVERSAL

P A R T
6

DRACULA

135  "The Master came and stood below my window and promised me things - - "

136  "- - not in words, but by making them happen!"

137  "A red mist spread over the lawn like a flame of fire - -"

138  "- - then he parted it and I could see thousands of rats and he seemed to be saying - - "

139  "Rats! Rats! Thousands - - millions of them - - and every one a life!"

140  "All these will I give you if you will obey me!"

141  "What did he want you to do?"

142  "That which has already been done!"

S.T.

143     "Strike me dead, Doctor, if he ain't torn them iron bars like they were cheese!"

144     "Dracula is in the house!"

145     "Martin - - put Renfield where he can't escape again."

146     "Come on, old fly-eater!"

147     "Van Helsing!"

148     "Now that you have learned what you have learned, it would be well to leave here at once."

149     "In intend to remain - - and protect those whom you would destroy!"

150     "You are too late! The blood of Dracula now flows through Mina's veins!"

151     "She will live though the centuries, even as I have lived!"

152     "We may not be able to save Mina's life - - but we do know how to save Miss Mina's soul - -"

153     "A stake through her heart!"

154     "If she dies by day! But I shall see that she dies by night!"

155     "Before you succeed, we will find your earth-boxes and drive a stake through your heart!"

156     "Come here!"

157     "Your will is strong, Van Helsing!"

158     "More wolfbane, Professor?"

159     "More effective than wolfbane!"

S.T.

160     "Miss Mina wouldn't go to bed - - she's out on the terrace."

161     "Why are you looking at me like that?"

162     "Mina! You're like a changed girl! You look wonderful!"

163     "I feel wonderful! I never felt better in my life!"

164     "Miss Mina - - you must come in-doors!"

165     "The fog's lifting!" How plainly you can see the stars!"

166     "Nothing is the matter. Come - - let's sit down!"

167     "Night is the only time when I feel really alive!"

168     "Yes!"

169     "I will!"

170     "You will what?"

171     "Why, I didn't say anything."

172     "That funny little professor - - he has a crucifix - - "

173     "- - I want you to get it and hide it."

174     "I'm sorry, Mina - - but I'm afraid we both misunderstand the professor."

175     "Give me that cross, Professor!"

176     "The cross! Put it away!"

177     "But what's happened - - tell me!"

| S.T. | |
|---|---|
| 178 | "Oh John! You must believe everything the Professor says! It's true - - Dracula - -" |
| 179 | "Dracula? What has he done to you?" |
| 180 | "He came to me. He opened a vein in his wrist |
| 181 | "What's wrong, Martin?" |
| 182 | "I took a shot at that big bat." |
| 183 | "No bullet of yours can kill that bat!" |
| 184 | "Ne's crazy!." |
| 185 | "They're all crazy except you an' me - -" |
| 186 | "And sometimes I have me doubts about you." |

U N I V E R S A L

END OF PART
6

DRACULA

---

U N I V E R S A L

P A R T
7

DRACULA

| | |
|---|---|
| 187 | "You will now retire - - and remember nothing." |
| 188 | "That's Renfield heading for Carfax Abbey! He may lead us to Dracula's earth-boxes!" |
| 189 | "I'm here, Master - - I'm here!" |
| 190 | "Mina! Mina! |

S.T.
191 "I didn't lead them here, Master - - I swear it!"

192 "No! No! Don't kill me, Master! Let me live!"

193 "The sun is rising! If we can keep Dracula in sight, he will lead us to his earth-box!"

194 "Here! Here! I've found them!"

195 "Get me a stone! Anything to drive a stake through their hearts!"

196 "Mina - - she is not here!"

197 "Then she may be alive!"

198 "Dracula had to go to his earth-box! The daylight saved me."

199 "At last Dracula is really dead - - a stake through his heart - - his soul at peace"

200 "And for you, too, the horror is over - -"

201     FADE IN PICTORIAL TRADE MARK
            T H E   E N D

   Whirling globe - ray of light - words appear

             IT'S A
           UNIVERSAL
            PICTURE

          ... FADE OUT

202     FADE IN - PICTORIAL CAST
       A GOOD CAST IS WORTH REPEATING
        Mina............HELEN CHANDLER
        Count Dracula.. BELA LUGOSI
        John Harker ....DAVID MANNERS
        Renfield ...... DWIGHT FRYE
        Van Helsing ... Edward van Sloan
        Dr. Seward .....Herbert Bunston
        Lucy .......... Francis Dade
        Maid ..........Joan Standing
        Martin ........Charles Gerrard

         U N I V E R S A L
          END OF PART 7
           DRACULA

# Appendix A

# NOSFERATU,
a symphony of horror
the
1922 Shooting Script

*(Above) Max Shreck takes a break during the shooting.*
*(Below) Hutter (Harker) meets Count Orlok (Dracula) disguised as a coachman*

114

NOSFERATU
by
Henrik Galeen
(F.W. Murnau's hand annotations and scenes additions and location markers are in Bold Print)
ACT 1

|  |  |
|---|---|
| Fade in. | 8 meters    location shot: Wismar<br>Townscape<br>View over the roof's of a small old-fashioned<br>town built in the style of the 1840s. The sun<br>shines peacefully on pointed gables and<br>leafy squares. |
| Fade out | Two shot, one from the church tower onto the town the<br>other from the harbour over towards the town.<br>1st: view of Lübeck.<br>Dissolve to harbour of Wismar |
| Scene 23<br>Fade-in<br>Outside a window | 4 meters    2x<br><br>There are flowers in green window-boxes. On the<br>window sill a kitten is playing in the morning sun.<br>With graceful movements she tries to catch a ball<br>that dangles from a thread. Now the ball is being<br>pulled in through the window. The cat jumps in<br>after it. |
| Scene 34<br>Small neat kitchen | **Ellen's sitting room    7 meters    2x**<br>The morning sun casts the shadow of a window<br>frame onto the floor. Ellen, by the window, is<br>pulling the thread with the ball, the cat follows it<br>with a leap. Then she puts the little animal on her<br>arm. **Playing with it she sits down on the window<br>sill bathed in sunshine and looks out dreamily.**<br>She squats on the floor opposite the animal and<br>plays with it. Her dressing gown moves in the breeze,<br>her big   child-like eyes a laughing. |
| Scene 34a<br>A small sitting room (attic) | **20 meters    Hutter    white jabot    blue waist coat.**<br>Poor-looking and tidy. A bed, a chair in the<br>period style. Hutter is standing in front<br>of the mirror. He is about to put his jack-<br>et on. He pauses to listen, takes a look<br>through the side window. Smiling happily<br>he finishes dressing and goes out. |
| 4a  A small flower garden | **Shot from above. Hutter appears, gardening<br>knife in hand, looks up    front of Hutter's house<br>beaming with joy. He finds a clump of carn-<br>ations, cuts the flowers with a quick gesture<br>and makes a bouquet.** |
| Scene 5<br>The small kitchen | Ellen, still playing with the kitten, hears Hutter<br>coming and jumps up. |

| | |
|---|---|
| Shot of cooker | Ellen comes over and begins to busy herself with the sauce pans, with a childlike earnestness towards her house-wifely duties. |
| Shot of door: | Hutter is standing in the doorway and laughs and laughs. **Hiding the bouquet behind his back, he laughs and laughs** |
| Shot of cooker | Ellen turns around, catches sight of her husband and seems a little ashamed that she hasn't yet made breakfast. Now Hutter moves closer to her, looks into the sauce pan holds it upside down indicating that it is empty, and looks at her reproachfully. |
| Title: | Ellen! |

She is sulking now and trying to placate him. But he pulls out his watch; it is late already; he has to go. He kisses her good-bye, but she calls him back again to confess that she hasn't got any money left to do the shopping. He pulls out his purse with a sad look and holds it up: there is nothing in it! They both sigh. He leaves with a heavy heart. The moment she is alone she takes a small basket of potatoes, which is all she can find, the last resort of the poor house-wife, and starts peeling them. A potato drops on the floor, the kitten comes up and plays with it.

| | |
|---|---|
| Fade-out | They are rushing towards each other, Ellen throws herself into Hutter's arms |
| Long Shot | He produces the bouquet, hands it to her beaming all over his face. She is touched then, saddening, she takes the glowers looking at the stems and stroking them. His voice asks for the reasons of her behavior she says: |
| Title | Why have you killed them ... the beautiful flowers? |

Hutter is taken aback for a moment. He apologizes and kisses her.
Then she forgives her, they stand in an embrace.

| | |
|---|---|
| Fade-out | 2x |
| Scene 5a<br>Fade in<br>Street with front gardens | 10 meters Lauenburg |
| Title: | Professor Bulwer |

Professor Bulwer is walking vigorously, yet slowly along the road, enjoying the morning and the sunshine. His stick strikes the ground energetically.
Suddenly he stops and turns around. Who is following him in such haste? Isn't it Hutter? He grasps the passing man by his sleeve; he holds on to it. Hutter greets him, looking pleased. Bulwer laughs and looking deep into his eyes says:

| | |
|---|---|
| Title: | Why so hasty, my young friend? One reaches one's goal soon enough. |

|  |  |
|---|---|
|  | Hutter, of course, doesn't understand him. He has to get to office quickly. He greets him again and again. Until he manages at last to break free with a laugh and rushes off. Bulwer stands there for a moment, then he resumes the regular rhythm of his walk. |
| **Scene 6**<br>Fade-in<br>Dusty cramped office | 6 meters Caption:  Knock - a house agent<br><br>Pale light is falling through tiny blind window-panes into the strange room which is eccentrically decorated with bits of old-fashioned furniture. KNOCK is standing at a high desk. People call him a house agent. |
| Close-up | Knock's spindly hunch-backed figure. Grey hair, weather-beaten face full of wrinkles. Around his mouth throbs the ugly tic of the epileptic. In his eyes burns a sombre fire. He is reading a letter. |
| Close-up | The letter. On a sheet of paper decorated on the margin with grotesque vignettes a medley of intricate and quite illegible signs. |
| Med. Close-up | Knock seems to be able to make sense of the strange letter, for his ugly mouth sets into an understanding smile. Then he turns and opens the door. |
| **Scene 7**<br>Small room adjoining the office | 5 meters<br><br>Very narrow and dark, totally without sun. Hutter, buried in files. Knock looks through the door and calls him in.<br>**Another clerk is present** |
| **Scene 8**<br>The dusty and cramped office | 30 meters<br><br>Knock and Hutter enter. Knock points to the letter with mysterious gestures and tells Hutter: |
| Title | Count Orlock - His grace - From Transylvania wants to buy a beautiful house in our little Town |
| Close-up | Knock's demonic face with wide open eyes |
| Title | You could make a nice bit of money . . .<br>It will take some effort, however . . .<br>a few drops of sweat and blood. . .<br>**Perhaps a little blood.** |
| Closeup | In Hutter's face expressions of mounting joy and strange apprehension are fighting each other. Yet joy wins in the end. |

| | |
|---|---|
| Long shot | Knock digs up and old atlas from the depths of the cabinet and opens it. His finger runs over a page. |
| Closeup | The route from England to Transyvania on the map. |
| Long shot | Transylvania? asks Hutter, his eyes suddenly shining at the thought of a journey. Yet Knock has turned back to the letter, now reading the last page. |
| Closeup | The back page of the letter, covered with the same illegible squiggles. |
| Long shot | Knock seems to be able to make sense of this page too. He turns back to Hutter who is already day-dreaming about his journey. |
| Title | He wants a handsome deserted house. |
| Long shot | For a moment Knock is lost in thought, then he has an idea. He limps over to the window. |
| **Scene 9**<br>Section of window | 4 meters   Window frame, take in Knock<br>View down the street<br>The deserted house. A dilapidated facade. Black and hollow windows. Not a sign of life. Shadows on it.<br>**Daytime - Sun** |
| **Scene 10**<br>The dusty and cramped office | 15 meters<br><br>Knock walks back from the window and says to Hutter: |
| Title | That house...just opposite yours.<br>Offer him that!<br><br>Hutter seems to be a little taken aback, but he rallies around quickly. Knock urges him to set out on the journey at once, hands him some money and documents and pushes him to the door. |
| Fade-out | 18 meters    2x   As in scene 8 |
| **Scene 11**<br>Room in Hutter's House | Ellen is sitting by the window. Now she can see him coming. She waves to him. Her face lights up with joy. She hurries over to the door. Presently Hutter enters. Moved and happy, he puts his arms around her and tells her his great news: |

| | |
|---|---|
| Title | I shall go on a journey far far away to the country of mountains where there are bandits and ghosts still. |
| | Ellen is startled. A shadow passes over her forehead. She wants to hold him back. But he is not listening. He has got to pack; already he is leaving her. |
| Fade-out Scene 12 The attic room Fade-in | 15 meters    Frau Schroeder without shawl    saddlebags |
| | Hutter is packing his little travelling bag. Ellen appears in the door behind him. Suddenly she starts to beg him tearfully, entreating: Do not go! I am worried about you! But he rejects her remonstrations. Now he has finished packing. He gets up. Ellen realizing that he has made up his mind steps back, resigning herself. But there is fear in her eyes. Seeing her like this he hesitates for a moment. But then he embraces her again with determination, takes up his bag and leaves the room with her. |
| **Fade out Scene 13** (Lord)Harding's park | 15 meters |
| | Hutter, all ready for the journey, takes his leave from Harding and his sister Anny. Ellen, weeping is supported by Anny. |
| Close-up | The two men. Hutter, taking both of Harding's hands and looking deep into his eyes: |
| Title | I entrust Ellen to your care. |
| | Harding promises his friend to look after Ellen, she can live here, she will never be alone. |
| Long shot of all characters | Hutter gives his hand to Anny and then to Ellen One last farewell kiss. At this moment her grief is over. As if she had a premonition she says: |
| Title | Farewell! There is no escape left. |
| | At first they are all startled by these words. Then Hutter breaks away. Another farewell, another wave of the hand and Hutter vanishes into the park. Ellen is staring vacantly into the distance. |

| | |
|---|---|
| Scene 14<br>Square with fountain | A number of healthy-looking people are walking about in the sunshine. Tied to the fountain a lonely sattled horse. Hutter appears, mounts the horse gives one last backward look and gallops off. |
| Fade out<br>Scene 15 | 9 meters Schlesische Hutte |
| Title | The Carpathian Mountains<br>Wild and rocky mountains. Contre jour |
| Fade-out | Evening |
| Scene 16<br>Long shot<br>Outside the Carpathian inn. | 10 meters |
| | The big mail coach drawn by four horses drives up and comes to a halt. |
| Shot of door of inn | The inn-keeper, a small old Jew, comes out and sees the coach. |
| Shot of coach: | Hutter jumps out first. He looks around. |
| Long shot: | The house. One part of brick-walled living area, the other coach house and open stables Shot of coach In the meantime the other passengers have got out. Long-haired, black Huzules. All identically dressed and of identical appearance like ghosts. they go into the house.<br><br>The inn-keeper has gone up to Hutter and greets him with an inviting gesture. |
| Shot of coach | The horses are now unharnessed, the coach is being pushed into the coach house. Night is falling. |
| Scene 17 | 8 meters   servant: Frau Kurz |
| Inside the Inn. | A large smoky room with an enormous tiled stove. A central hanging lamp throws out dazzling light At tables in the background the passengers. Hutter who came in last, is standing in the foreground, he looks around and sits down right in front. At once the old servant approaches with a glass and puts it down in front of him. He overcomes a strange anxiety that was brought on by the evening mood in a strange country and puts on a sudden show of liveliness. He knocks on the table and says: |
| Title | Quickly, my meal -<br>I must be off to Count Orlock's<br>castle. |
| | The servant recoils in horror. The strangely identical looking passengers, sitting in the background rise up abruptly to stare at him. |
| Shot of bar | The old hunch-backed Jew pricks up his ears. |

| | | |
|---|---|---|
| Long shot | | Hutter looks around in embarrassment, then takes up his glass resolutely and downs it in one gulp. |
| **Scene 18** A grassy slope behind the inn | 4 meters | Walddorfsenke The ground falls away towards the back. Night mists are creeping up from the valley. The horses are put out here to graze. Suddenly, they raise their heads, as if frightened and, scattering, gallop away. |
| **Scene 19** Inside the inn Shot of window: | | The passengers, seen from behind are standing by the window, looking out apprehensively. The old servant has not go the courage to go up to where they stand and makes the sign of the cross. Hutter stands alone, looking around. He is perplexed and wants to ask what is happening. The old servant comes up to him and whispers into his ear. |
| Title | | You mustn't go there now there are wolves about Spend the night here. |
| | | Hutter understands and decides to stay. |
| Fade-out 19a | | **Hyena** |
| 19b | | **Horses, panicking** |
| **Scene 20** A room at the inn. | 6 meters | A tiny white-washed room with sharp angles: a flickering light from the old servant's candle. Now Hutter enters. She puts the candle down, goes out without a word. Her eyes expressing concern for him. Hutter alone. He goes over to the window, throws it open and looks into the starless night. |
| **Scene 21** | | (missing from script) |
| **Scene 22** Inside the inn | 5 meters | The pale passengers, now without Hutter in the enormous room, look frightened. They, too, are listening to the horrible howling. They look at each other and are crossing themselves in terror! |
| **Scene 23** The tiny white-washed room | 20 meters | In the light of the candle Hutter, shivering, closes the window. He is no longer sleepy. He walks up and down the room restlessly, stopping in front of a little bookcase. |
| Medium close-up | | Looking for something to distract him Hutter pulls out a book at random. |
| Long shot | | He moves back to the candle, sits down on his bed and opens the book. He gets interested in it. |
| Close up | | The book's title page: VAMPIRE The page os being turned over. THE NOSFERATU From the bloody sins of mankind a creature will be born which will seek revenge for the sin committed by the parents and visited on their children and children's children. Whosoever lusts after blood without reason in under his spell, the spell of the vampire NOSFERATU. |

| | |
|---|---|
| Shot of bed Close-up | **Hutter, shaking his head, continues reading Book:...grown up on his native soil - from which alone he draws his power.** |
| | Hutter shuts the book, having lost interest. It seems confused to him. He yawns and puts out the candle. |
| Fade-out | |
| **Scene 24** | **12 meters** |
| Fade-in Small white room at the inn | Morning sun is flooding in from the window. Hutter wakes up. Yawning like someone who has slept deeply but not well. He sits up rubbing his eyes. They fall on the book on the bedside table. He reads the title |
| Close-up Normal shot: | VAMPIRE spits on the floor in contempt of the confused rubbish and throws the book playfully into a corner. Then he pauses to listen, goes over to the window to open it. He takes a deep breath of the morning air. |
| Scene 25 | **6 meters    Walddorf** The grassy slope in the morning light. Coachmen and grooms are rounding up the horses with long whips and lots of shouting. |
| Scene 26 The small room | **5 meters** Hutter steps back from the window. His eyes are laughing, as he turns round. He stretches himself happily; then he takes off his shirt, goes over to the washstand, pours water over his body. He has a proper wash. |
| Scene 27 In the yard | **Dolny Kubin** The old servant, mother to all animals, throws corn to her chickens. There are sparrows, too. Everything is bathed in sunlight. |
| Scene 28 Outside the Inn | **10 meters** The bustle of departure. The horses are in harness. The passengers have got into the coach. Now, in the morning light, one can see their differences. They are much less uniform than they had seemed the previous nightfall. They are chattering noisily to the people who are staying behind and with the peasants and nosy children who are gathered around the coach. |
| Close-up | The coachman is about to climb onto his seat, but the small Jewish inn-keeper holds him back: one passenger is missing. They look up to the windows; angry about the delay the coachman cracks his whip a few times. |
| Shot of inn: | Hutter appears in an upstairs window, still only half dressed; he gives a wave: I am coming. And disappears again. |
| Shot of door | Hutter comes rushing out with his travelling bag. |

| | |
|---|---|
| Shot of coach | He climbs to his seat on the coach-box, the horses start moving. |
| Scene 29<br>Outside the inn | The Huzules take off their hats. The children are waving. The old servant has joined them. God bless the travellers. May he guard them against evil spirits. They stretch out their hands as if warding them off. |
| Medium close-up<br>Fade-out | Hutter breaks into loud laughter. |
| Scene 30 | 12 meters        Westerheim |
| A Mountain range<br>Long-range shot | In the distance a steep path cutting through the wild scenery, on it the mail coach creeping slowly upwards. |
| Scene 31<br>The mail coach | 10 meters    road to the Schlesische Hütte |
| Medium close-up<br>Medium close-up | The mail coach is moving into the setting sun<br>A coach window, and old woman. Hutter leans out, giving the coachman a push with an umbrella |
| Title | Drive on! |
| The sun is setting | Next to her another old woman, identical looking She is staring into the abyss. Now the first one turns to look in the same direction: two identical faces. |
| Scene 32 | 4 meters    View from Schlesische Hütte |
| The rocky gorge | Wisps of mist are rising and falling in the last rays of the setting sun. Patches of sun and shade |
| Fade-out<br>Scene 33 | 10 meters    Close to Arler Hütte |
| Title | At the crossroad |
| | A carved madonna casts a long shadow across the road. Behind it an old woman on her knees, deep in prayer. She lifts her head and looks down the road. The mail coach approaches, the horses are pulling with difficulty, breathing hard. She seems to ask herself: do they want to drive to the haunted castle? and gets into the middle of the road to warn them off. The mail coach stops. Hutter gets off the coach box. Now he stands at the crossroad. The passengers are anxious to move on gesturing violently to him not to take the left fork. But Hutter disregards their shouting He waves farewell with his hat and walks briskly off. |
| **33a** | **Hutter walking past the carved madonna** |

**Scene 34**
Distant mountains

**8 meters    Vratna Pass**
View through the cut made into the rock by the road into the far distance. In the background the fantastic castle of Count Orlok in the evening light. One can see a steep road leading straight up into the sky. Something comes racing down. A coach? A phantom? It moves with unearthly speed and disappears behind a ground swell.

**1) Castle Orlok, dissolve**
**2) Steep road between boulders**

**Scene 35**
At the crossroad
Angle as in Scene 33

**4 meters    Near Schlesische Hütte**

Mortally fightened, the coachman beats the horses. The old woman has disappeared as if swallowed up by the ground. Astonished, Hutter follows the vanishing coach with his eyes. He is all alone now, standing like this for a while. Then he pulls himself together and walks resoltuely along the road on the left.

Fade-out
**Scene 36**
Fade-in
Carpathian virgin forest.

**Vratna Pass**

The trees are castling long shadows on the forest path. Hutter appears. He halts: what's that? Something comes racing up, turns around as if moved by a hidden force and moving jerkily. Stops dead. Hutter likewise. A black carriage. No wheels? Two black horses - griffins? Their legs are invisible, covered by a black funeral cloth. Their eyes like pointed stars. Puffs of steam from their open mouths, revealing white teeth. The coachman is wrapped up in black cloth. His face pale as death. His eyes are staring at Hutter. Raising his whip he makes an inviting, almost commanding gesture. He waits. Hutter cannot rally enough strength to follow the invitation. Yet those eyes assert their power. Step by step, as if pulled by invisible threads, Hutter approaches the uncanny creature. He gets into the carriage. It reverses quick as lightning, dashes off a disappears.

**Scene 37**
A fairy-tale forest

**5 meters    At the Vratna Pass, behind Tyer Hora**
Empty. By the roadside a wise, man-sized raven. Its shoulders hunched up. It turns its head listening. Then takes two hops forward and looks down the road. Who's coming? The familiar vehicle sweeps up and past. A young man, holding on desperately, sits inside, looking terrified. **The raven** follow him with mocking eyes behind glasses.
**Coach drives at top speed through a white forest**

**Scene 38**
Long shot of a snake-like bend.

**5 meters**

Valley. Deserted lane. Only a lonely twisted will-tree with a straggly top can be seen. Again the carriage races past. Like an ancient man who has been disturbed in his rest the tree looks after the vehicle with blank eyes. Isn't there a grin on its mouth? Drives over stone bridge across deep gorge

| | | |
|---|---|---|
| Scene 39<br>Count Orlock's castle<br>39a | **15 meters   Poczamok** | |
| | The arch of a gate in the shade. The silhouette of the carriage drives underneath it at a sharp angle and disappears in the moonlit spacious castle yard. Shot of castle yard | |
| Medium close-up | The porch. The carriage stops in front of it. Almost in a faint, Hutter slides down. As if in a whirlpool, the carriage circles round him and disappears. Hutter turns around and follows it with his eyes. He stands in front of the closed gate, holding his bag. | |
| 39b | Then, very very slowly the two wings of the gate open up. Somewhere far back in the dark corridor a man can be seen standing motionless. He is holding a candle which lights up his chalk-white face. He is waiting. Who is that? Hutter bounds up the two steps and stands in the doorway. He would still like to go back. Yet it is too late now. Hesitantly he walks towards the stranger. Behind him the gate closes | |

**End of Act 1**

Act II

Scene 40
Hall.
Medium close-up — In the center Orlok, the candle in his hand. The walls of the hall are plunged in darkness from which Hutter's back emerges. He faces the motionless figure. It is pale, ghostly creature with hollow eyes and thin mouth the lord of the castle himself?

Close-up — The face twists into a polite grimace. Sharp ratlike teach appear over the lower lip.

Medium Close-up — They are now face to face. It must be the count for this is no servant's gesture with which he now takes hold of his visitor's bag.

Title — The servants are asleep
It is almost after midnight.

Hutter's clenched fingers let go. Bag in hand, Orlok turns around. He holds up the candle and walks ahead. Hutter follows.

Scene 41
Gallery of ancestor's portraits
Medium Close-up — One of the castle owner's ancestors, frontal view. For centuries he has been asleep like this with his eyes closed. Now something approaches. His eyes begin to move. Two figures are passing: Orlok and his visitor.

Long shot panorama — He follows them with his eyes. They walk close to the wall where portrait follows portrait.

Scene 42
Dining room.
25 meters
Gigantic dimensions. In the center a massive Renaissance table. Somewhere in the distance a fire place. Flanked by two armoured figures. Black and motionless. In older times this must have been used by knights for their drinking bouts. Are these their armour? Is that long line that runs across the wall a crack in the old structure? Or a lance left hanging there? Suddenly, Hutter notices that the count is waiting. Quickly he hands him the plans of the deserted house and Knock's letters. With a smile Orlok takes them and begs him to take a seat. The meal is waiting. Hutter sits down. Orlok lifts up the papers and studies them.

Close-up — Orlok reading. The back page of the letter shows a confusion of numbers, legible and illegible letters. The holy number seven is repeated several times. In between, cabbalistic signs. The spindly fingers holding the letter cover up the rest like claws.

Close-up — Hutter is spell bound, his eyes wide-open

Closeup — Over the top margin of the letter Orlok's eyes appear. He is looking over to Hutter like a snake about to hypnotize it's victim.

Close-up — Hutter eating. He puts a morsel into his mouth. He lifts up his eyes. His look turns into a stare. He is unable to swallow

| | |
|---|---|
| Long shot | The hall with the halo of light in the center; the figures are looming above the table. |
| Close-up | An antique clock with a pendulum. A hammer strikes the hour. The big hand points to 12 o'clock. |
| Medium close-up: | Hutter staring into space as if transfixed. After the twelfth stroke he drops his knife and fork. The knife grazes his hand, it is bleeding. |
| Medium Close-up | Quick as lightning the count rushes up to him offering his help. He prevents Hutter from wiping off the blood. The knife might have been poisoned The sticky blood should be removed from the cut. His lips are sucking at the hand hastily. Frightened, Hutter pulls away his hand from his grip. He moves backwards **towards the fireplace.** |
| Medium Close-up | By the fireplace. The Count is polite; he has lost his ghostlike appearance. He is asking for something in a friendly, almost sad manner. |
| Title | Shall we stay up together for a little while? It's a long time to go till sunrise . . . And during the day I am always out and about. |
| | The Count sits down. And Hutter cannot resist his chivalrous manner. He sinks back into the massive chair. |
| Scene 43 Fade-in | **18 meters** |
| The same hall | Hutter wakes up in the large armchair near the fireplace. He can hardly remember the events of the night. The armchair opposite seems to be empty. But there is light on it. Hutter's gaze wanders across the hall over to the window. |
| Shot of window | It is very high and divided up into small panes. Morning light is streaming in. |
| Shot as before | An old-fashioned window. An ancient hall, very dusty. Nothing strange about it. Hutter yawns. His eyes fall on the cut in his hand and he remembers a few more things. What has he got on his neck? He touches his throat. Must have been mosquitoes. A mirror! His bag is nearby on the floor. He takes out his mirror and looks at his neck. |
| Close-up | The mirror shows two red spots on his neck, very close together. |
| Normal close-up | Why should he worry about a few little spots? he thinks and puts the mirror away. He yawns once more. But suddenly he stops. What's this? He looks at the table, astonished. |

| | |
|---|---|
| Close up: | A still-life of food: fruit, a joint, all kinds of gastronomic delicacies. |
| Normal: | He is overjoyed. He rushes over to the table and begins to eat as if he were starved. |

**Scene 44**
The dilapidated terrace

22 meters    Poczamok
Still eating, Hutter steps out into the sunlight. He looks around, seeming relaxed. He holds a sheet of paper and a pencil in his hands. Then he casts about for a suitable place and, leaning against the stone wall He begins to write a letter.

| | |
|---|---|
| Close-up: | The beginning of the letter: My dearest, my only one... |
| Normal: | Hutter stands upright, looking at the clouds. Why does that stupid mosquito buzzing around his nose stop him from concentrating? He catches it quickly. And now he knows how to continue. He puts pencil to paper again. |
| Close-up: | Part of the letter:...the mosquitoes are a real pest. I have been stung at the next by two at once, very close together, one on each side... |
| Long shot: | Hutter keeps writing |

**Scene 45**
Forest near the castle

14 meters    Poczamok
A man on horseback is approaching. He stops occasionally and peers over to the castle as if he were scared of it.

| | |
|---|---|
| Outside the porch: | Hutter stands there, waving with the letter. The rider comes up cautiously and takes the letter without dismounting The he dashes off at a gallop showing signs of great fear. |

**Scene 46**
Fade-in.
Dining room

15    meters

Orlok is sitting by the fireplace bent over some plans. Hutter is standing behind him. Orlok shows more interest in the young man than in the papers lying in front of him. Looking over his shoulder he asks for some more information. Hutter rummages among the papers in his bag. A little picture falls on the table. He wants to hide it quickly, yet Orlok was quicker. He has picked it up and is looking at it.

| | |
|---|---|
| Close up | A miniature portrait of Ellen. |
| Medium close-up | Orlock asks about the person in the picture. And Hutter is forced to answer him. |
| Close up: | Orlok's eyes open wide. His lips look even thinner than before. Contemplating the picture he whispers: |
| Title | What a beautiful throat your wife has... |

| | |
|---|---|
| Medium close-up: | Hutter is breathing hard. The fear which grips him in the count's presence is replaced by a sudden fear for his wife. He forgets himself and reaches for the miniature. For the first time he touches Orlok's body. The count jumps up. He raises himself to his full height with triumphant determination and a glazed look in his eyes, and says, anticipating the horrors to come with pleasure. |
| Title | I shall buy the house... The handsome deserted house opposite yours. |
| | Quickly, he takes up the contract and signs it. He hands it back to Hutter. Hutter bows uneasily and retires. Orlok watches him go, a satanic look has come into his eyes. His hands have turned into claws. **Hutter takes his bag with him** |
| Fade-out: | |
| **Scene 47** Fade-in: A small room in castle | **15 meters** **Candle is burning** Hutter is standing in the middle of the room, quite dazed. He shakes off his misgivings. He decides to leave tomorrow. He kisses the picture and starts to undress, when to his amazement he discovers a book in his pocket. The old book from the inn. Did the in-keepers wife put it there? Mechanically, he opens it. |
| Close-up: | The book Chapter II Night is the vampire's element. He can see in the dark which is a wonderful ability to have in this world half of which is night. We humans, however, are helpless and blind at night |
| Normal | Hutter shuts the book. A horrible thought has occurred to him. He is feverish. Is it this book, these ancient walls which make him believe in the existence of ghosts? Did not the count seem to have vampire-like claws and rat's teeth. He jumps up, first running, the sneaking to the door. |
| **Scene 48** Dining hall View from door deep into the dining hall | **4 meters** By the fireplace Count Orlok, no, not Orlock but a gigantic vampire, a motionless, sombre watcher in the night. |
| Medium close-up | He looks at Hutter with a fixed glaze. |

| | |
|---|---|
| Scene 49<br>The small room.<br>Shot of door: | **6 meters**<br><br>Hutter. He supports himself against the doorpost. A terrible realization has dawned on him. Shut the door, shut it quickly! There is no bolt. No lock. He looks around, puts the heavy oak-chair against the door. Is it possible to escape? |
| Medium close-up: | Window. Hutter rushes up and flings it open. |
| Scene 50 | **3 meters    Tegeler Forest**<br>Night. Undergrowth. A pack of wolves, raising their heads howling. |
| Scene 51<br>The small room<br>Long shot: | **8 meters**<br><br>Hutter falls on his knees by the side of the bid. Hutter clutching the bedclothes, he stares at the door behind which the horror is waiting.<br>What is this? |
| Medium close-up: | Moved by an invisible hand the door opens to half its width in one single jerk. |
| Long shot: | Hutter. Terrified, he covers his eyes with his arms, pulls at the bedclothes and shields his eyes. He mustn't see it. He mustn't look! |
| Fade out.<br>Scene 52<br>Title | **6 meters**<br>The same night |
| Ellen's bedroom at the Hardings | She wakes up suddenly. She has been dreaming. As if she had seen a vision ... She has a premonition of danger ... Now she gets up. Moves over to the window and steps out on to the balcony. |
| Scene 53<br>Harding's study | **6 meters**<br>Night. Harding is sitting at his desk. He hears a noise Rushes out. |
| Scene 54<br>Ellen's bedroom<br>Medium close-up of door leading to the balcony | Ellen is perching on the edge of the balcony. Harding rushes into the room. Discovers that the bed is empty. He shouts: Ellen! |
| Title | Ellen!<br><br>He catches sight of the sleepwalker at the moment when, woken up by his shouts, she loses her balance and falls over. He runs up to her and gathers her in his arms. He carries her over to the bed. A servant, alerted by the noise appears in the door. A doctor! shouts Harding. The servant disappears. |

| | |
|---|---|
| Scene 55<br>Fade-in.<br>The small castle room<br>Long Shot | 6 meters<br><br>Hutter in bed, tense and doubled up. Slowly, Nosferatu creeps up on him.<br>Irresistible, he bends over the terrified and helpless man and buries his fangs in his throat. |
| Fade-out.<br>Scene 56<br>Fade in.<br>Ellen's bedroom<br>Long shot: | 7 meters<br><br><br><br>Ellen shouts: |
| Title | Hutter!!! |
| Long shot: | Ellen in bed ...in delirium. Anny is kneeling by her side. A doctor. Professor Sievers, is taking her pulse. Harding<br>Ellen trembles like a wounded bird. She doubles up throws herself about and retreats into a corner of the bed. |
| Scene 57<br>The small castle room<br>Medium close-up | 8 meters<br>Night<br>NOSTERATU turns his head. He is listening intently as if he could feel - hear the **terrified** shouting in the distance. |
| Long shot | NOSTERATU moves away from Hutter's bed. He dissolves into the air! **leaves the room** |
| Scene 58 | 8 meters |
| Ellen's bedroom<br><br>Medium close-up: | Ellen is calming down slowly. Her terror turns into apathy. Breathing weakly.<br>She settles back listlessly into her pillows. Sievers can tell the improvement from the pulse-rate and says to Harding: |
| Title: | Normal congestion of the blood. . .<br>caused by an awkward position<br>during sleep...<br><br>He has assumed an academic air. His beard trembles in his eagerness. |
| Fade-out. | |
| Scene 59 | 3 meters  Poczamok<br>Behind a pointed gable of the castle the sun is rising slowly. |
| Fade-out.<br>Scene 60<br>Fade-in.<br>The small castle room | 7 meters<br><br><br>The light of dawn is falling through the window as though a sky-light and moving along the wall until it reaches Hutter's face, looking half-faint-ing, half asleep.<br>Suddenly he wakes up |

| | |
|---|---|
| Scene 60 continued | He starts up and clutches his throat. He jumps out of bed, clenching his fists, runs over. To the door. Carefully ...he looks out |
| Scene 61<br>Dining hall | **6 meters**<br>Daytime.<br>The room is empty ...Hutter, pale and hollow-eyed, staggers in. He looks around ...nothing. Shaking his head, fists clenched with wild determination, he drags himself forward. |
| Scene 62<br>Portrait gallery with flight of stairs | **6 meters**<br><br>Hutter is dragging himself along with difficulty. He goes down a few stairs. At the end of the corridor he finds a door. He opens it. |
| **62a. A curving gallery exterior** | **Hutter opens one door after the other** |
| Scene 63<br><br>A vault | **15 meters**<br><br>Empty and dark.<br>In the center of the darkness a black coffin. Hutter has pushed the door open and enters. He starts back. He stares without understanding. Fear grips him. But he must make certain. Trembling heavily, he lifts up the coffin lid. He recoils in horror. Dropping the lid, he retreats into the darkest corner. For inside the coffin he has seen, black and long, the lifeless body of NOSFERATU. Horror-stricken, Hutter almost collapses. Then he rushes out. |
| Fade-out.<br>Scene 64<br>Fade in.<br>Sunset. | **3 meters   Poczamok   Vratna Pass   Tatra**<br><br>Between a line of bizarre tree-trunks evening approaches like a ghost... |
| Scene 65<br>Fade-in.<br>A niche inside the castle | **6 meters**<br><br>**The small castle room**.<br>Hutter is crouched on the floor. His body is twisted with fear. His hair is standing on end ...his eyes are staring. Suddenly, he starts up and listens. Can he hear a noise in this desolate place? Could it mean his salvation? With difficulty he drags his weakened body over to the window. |
| Scene 66<br><br>The walls of the castle seen from outside | Window frame for out-door shot<br>**3 meters   Poczamok**<br><br>Hutter stares from a window.<br>He refuses to believe what he sees.<br>**The crossbar of a window** |
| Scene 67 | **[12] meters 6 meters        Poczamok**<br>One can see a low-wheeled cart with the two fantastic horses harnessed to it. And now: is it a shadow? A ghost. Nosferatu. He is moving to and fro, to and fro. From the cart to the castle. And back again. Carrying boxes. Black coffin like boxes. From the back door of the castle to the carriage He piles them up. Box on box. Into a gigantic pyramid. All this happens at an uncanny speed. |

| | |
|---|---|
| Scene 68<br>Part of the castle wall | **3 meters Poczamok**<br>Hutter, staring at the phantom with glazed eyes. |
| Scene 69<br>Castle yard | **6 meters Poczamok**<br>The carriage is now loaded. Suddenly the phantom jumps on to the topmost box and disappears inside it. Instantly the horses dash off with the cart at lightning speed. The big gate closes behind them with a bang. |
| Scene 70<br>The small castle room | **8 meters**<br>Hutter jumps back from the window. |
| Title | Ellen! |

NOSFERATU is on his way. Ellen is in danger. He has to hurry. Save Ellen. Ellen! Ellen!. Suddenly, he starts tearing down the wall-hangings and tearing **up the bedclothes**. He tears them making long pieces and knotting them into a rope.

Fade-out.

| | |
|---|---|
| Scene 71<br>The abyss | **10 meters Poczamok**<br>Hutter dangling from a window in the castle walls on a rope. But the rope is too short.<br>Beneath him, the abyss still opens up.<br>And yet he risks the drop - dead or alive. |
| Medium close-up. | So he hurls himself down. Hutter is lying at the bottom of the abyss, between trees and boulders. Tossing and turning in fever and pain. So he tries to lift himself up. But pain seizes him again. Then he faints. |
| Scene 72<br>Fade-in.<br>By the river Pruth<br>**Waag** | **10 meters** |
| | The river flows majestically through the immense plain. The scenery is bathed in sunshine.<br>All is peaceful.<br>Then a large raft appears around a bend in the river and gloats slowly into view. Boatmen with long poles are pushing it with considerable effort. At the stern a high pile of boxes. Black, coffin like boxes. Stacked into a pyramid. An uncanny sight. Indefatigably, the boatmen go on punting The raft is coming closer and closer - like doom. |
| Fade-out. | |

**End of Act II**

## Act III

| | |
|---|---|
| Scene 73 | **12 meters** |
| Title | A Budapest hospital |
| Hospital Ward | A long line of white beds.<br>In the foreground, Hutter. In bandages ...<br>his eyes closed.<br>The doctor comes to him now.<br>He examines him. Questions the nurse<br>She tells him about the case: |
| Title | He was brought in yesterday<br>by Huzules who said he had<br>fallen down a mountain.<br>He is still feverish ... |
| | As the doctor continues his examination Hutter wakes<br>up, opens his eyes.<br>There is fear in his feverish look still.<br>The nurse hurries up to him to hold him.<br>Yet he crawls away to the end of the bed.<br>Spreads out his hands to defend himself.<br>Suddenly his eyes go dead. He collapses.<br>His lips are murmuring something ...<br>The doctor bends over to hear what he is saying.<br>Hutter muttering to himself |
| Title | Coffins - - - |
| Medium close-up: | Doctor and nurse look at each other without<br>understanding. |
| Fade-out.<br>Scene 74<br>Fade-in.<br>The port of Varna | **18 meters**<br><br>At the quayside, ready for loading, and next to other cargo<br>the pile of black coffins. Custom officials are examining<br>the lettering and papers. They are approaching the boxes.<br>The man searches among the papers and hands over the<br>freight letters to his boss. |
| Close-up: | Freight letter<br>**Mixed cargo, from Varna to Whitby**<br>**Content: garden soil for experimental purposes.** |
| Normal shot: | The inspector smiles incredulously. He orders a search!!<br>Barefooted dock-workers drag up one of the apparently<br>very heavy boxes, heaving and swearing. The inspector<br>gives an order.<br>They open the lid with difficulty. There is **earth** inside!<br>The inspector gives another order: turn it out! The workers<br>obey. Sand is falling out nothing but **earth**.<br>Satisfied, the inspector turns to another pile of cargo.<br>Yet in the earth . . .something moves violently ...something is<br>alive ...jumps out...horrible animals ...rats! One of the dock<br>workers, who bends over to scoop the scatters earth back<br>hits out violently. Did not one of the animals...reeling from<br>the blow ... bite his foot? |

| | |
|---|---|
| Long shot: | The big **hand pulley** [steam crane] hauls up one of the boxes and drops it into the belly of the sailing-boat that is anchored at the quay. At the ship's stern one can discern a name, underneath the baroque figure head; DEMETER |
| Scene 75<br>Title | **12 meters**<br>Professor Bulwer, a Paracelsian, explains the nature of carnivorous plants to his students |
| The institute<br>Medium close-up: | Professor Bulwer, surrounded by a few students, quiet and simple people. They are listening to his lecture. Now he points emphatically to a plant with a very strange shape. |
| Close-up: | A flower. Its petals reaching out like tentacles. Motionless. Now. And insect. Hovering, attracted by the scent . . . settles on the colorful calyx. There in a flash the tentacles have gripped it. The insect is caught. Its struggling is in vain. With irresistible force the flower has drawn it into the recesses of the calyx . . . |
| Medium- close-up: | Bulwer pointing at the flower. Slowly his lips are moving: |
| Title: | The patient who came in yesterday has had an attack. |
| Scene 77<br>Lunatic's cell | **12 meters**<br>Sievers and the attendant stop short at the door way. Straining their eyes to see into the semi-darkness. There, in the corner. Something moves slowly. It is a man. Now his face is in the light. Like a panther preparing to leap, his ferocity restrained, he raises himself up slowly. His crazed burning eyes staring at Sievers. And now we recognize him at last . . . it is Knock!!!<br>Suddenly, in one leap, he is at the window. Sievers is startled, says something to the attendant. Who prepares the straitjacket be brought along.<br>Yet the expected attack does not come.<br>Knock remains at the window, arms jerking, he begins . . . to catch flies which he puts into his mouth. Horrible food. The madman's face twists into a grin that resembles distant lightning. His swollen lips are murmuring something: |
| Title: | Blood is life! Blood is life!!!<br><br>Suddenly, the madman starts up and throws himself with all his might on the unsuspecting Sievers. Who can barely ward him off. But the attendant comes to his help quickly and throws the straightjacket over the raging man's head. |

| | |
|---|---|
| Scene 78<br>The Institute: | **8 meters**<br>Bulwer, in a quiet, scholarly manner with his students. He points to an aquarium. |
| Close-up: | On a piece of rock in the water hangs a small polyp. Now it stretches out its tentacles, grabs a small fish and pulls it up to its mouth. It is almost transparent, colorless and of a jelly-like consistency. |
| Title: | And this one . . .a polyp with tentacles . . .<br>transparent . . . almost incorporeal . . .<br>almost a phantom . . . |
| Scene 79<br>Lunatic's cell.<br>Close-up | **8 meters**<br><br>On the floor, in his straitjacket, whining pitifully, mad Knock. His face. Turning his sad eyes upwards. He notices something there. His lips form a word: |
| Title: | Spiders . . . ! |
| Close-up: | A spider-web with a live spider which clutches, vampire-like an insect and is sucking its blood. |
| Normal: | Knock in exultation.<br>Sievers stands motionless . . . does not understand.<br>Brusquely, he gives an order and leaves. |
| Fade-out.<br>Scene 80 | **4 meters** |
| Fade in.<br>The graveyard of<br>Whitby | <br><br>View from the pier-head towards the shore. In the foreground the surging sea. Further back, where the shore rises steeply, the graveyard of Whitby. |
| Closer: | The graveyard. Afternoon light. In front of the graveyard a long row of benches. People are strolling up and down looking out on to the sea . . . sitting on the benches and enjoying the view. |
| Medium close-up: | A bench, somewhat apart from the others. Ellen is sitting there. Dreamily, her eyes searching a distant country beyond the sea. She seems to be in an anxious daydream about her distant lover. Now she shuts her eyes, because tears are welling up. |
| Scene 81 | **4 meters**   Croquet? |
| In Harding's Park | Harding, youthful and athletic, is batting. The shuttlecock flies high up into the air. Anny, in a light dress, shouts with joy . . . catches it . . . throws it back. The shuttlecock flies backwards and forwards. It is a picture of health and light. |

| | |
|---|---|
| Scene 82<br>At the park gates. | **6 meters**<br>The postman, a small old man, rummages in his leather bag and produces a letter which he hands with an air of importance to Harding's servant who is as old and wizened as he. Before he leaves, the postman points to the stamp which seems to be of special value, lifting up his eyebrows: This letter has travelled ar . . . it comes from a very remote country. The two old men bend over the rare letter. Then the old servant takes it in. |
| Scene 83<br>In the park | **6 meters**<br>As the servant approaches. Harding and Anny stop playing. Anny takes the letter, reads the address and runs to her brother. It is for Ellen, she says, pointing into the distance. Shall we take it to her straight away. Harding agrees, they hand their rackets over to the ser- and walk off. |
| Scene 84<br>At the graveyard<br>Medium close-up: | **3 meters**<br><br>Ellen is still sitting there, looking over the vast waters, lost in her sad longing thoughts. |
| Scene 85<br>The sea | **3 meters**   **Heligoland**<br>Distant view over the sea. A sand bank skirted by rocks, jutting out into the surf waters. |
| Scene 86<br>At the graveyard. | **12 meters**<br>Harding and Anny are approaching. They are joining the lonely Ellen. shaking hands and trying to cheer her up. Guess what we have brought you! They show her the letter. Ellen trembles. She takes the letter quickly and tries to open it! I cannot do it. Gladly and quickly, Anny takes over. You'll see, he is safe and sound and sends you good news. She starts to read it gives a joyful laugh, she was right. All is well. The worries were unfounded Happily she gives Ellen the letter. But barely has she read the letter when Ellen's face assumes an expression of hurt certainty. Does she derive evil premonitions from these lines? |
| Close up: | The letter.<br>the mosquitoes are a real pest. I have been stung on the neck by two at once, very close together, one on each side . . . |

Normal: Ellen's face is distorted as if she were suffering physical pain. Harding and Anny are perplexed.

Scene 87
Title: GALAZ
The port of Galaz
at night.

The 'Demeter' is anchored off the jetty. Nobody is about on the quay. A stormy night, strange uncertain light. Suddenly - a gentle movement from the ship down the gangway to the shore . . . rats . . .

Fade-out: **The coffins are reloaded**
Scene 88 **10 meters**
The hospital at Budapest Hutter, dressed, stands in front of his bed. He looks pale and weak still, yet full of resolution. The nurse notices his unsteady stance. She fusses around him. You ought to stay a few more days! Have some more rest! But he wards her off. His gestures are restless and fluttering, a strange force has taken possession of him.

Title: I have to get home by
the shortest possible way!!

So he says goodbye, disregarding the nurse's advice, thanks her for her care and goes out quickly.

Scene 89

Title: Constantinople

The port. Night. Wild dogs are barking from the debris in the street up to the distant firmament, writhing in the mud like snakes.

Focus on quay: The "Demeter" at anchor. What's scuttling over there? . . . A shadow from the ship to the land . . . rats. . . one. . . four. . . ten . . . and endless stream . . .the carry terror with them.

Scene 90 **8 meters   Polnischer Kamm   Non-stop rain**
**Entry to the Vratna Gorge**

Title: In the Hungarian plain.

Coach station in the Pusta The mail coach is arriving at top speed. The coachman whips his exhausted horses into a last effort. The coach has barely stopped when Hutter jumps off. He calls for more speed. Now fresh horses are being brought along.
Hutter joins the grooms and tells them to hurry on! To hurry on!
The tired horses have been taken out of harness and are being led to the stable. Bring fresh horses! Hutter gives a helping hand. Now the straps are done up. The coachman blows his horn. Some late-comers appear. They get into the coach. Hutter is the last. And the heavy coach rumbles off, the horses galloping, sparks flying from the hooves, dust rising, into the pathless country.

Fade-out. **Hutter leads a limping horse through**

| | |
|---|---|
| Scene 91<br>Fade-in:<br>The port of Constantiople<br>Long shot. | In a fresh breeze, the "Demeter" emerges from the confusion of mast-heads and gains the open sea. |
| Scene 92<br>Lunatic's cell | **15 meters**<br>In a stupor, Knock is perching on his bunk. The attendant holding a broom, is about to leave the cell. At this moment Knock lifts his eyes. With a look of artful cunning and with rigid concentration he follows the attendant's movements. Now, he seems to have discovered an opportunity; softly, he sneaks up on the unsuspecting man and takes away the newspaper that sticks out of his pocket. The attendant does not notice and shuts the door behind him. The moment Knock is alone he unfolds the paper trembling with expectancy and starts reading. searching for something with wide-open eyes. Now he has found what he was looking for. He is riveted to this passage. |
| Close-up: | The Newspaper<br><br>              PLAGUE<br>In Transyvania and in the Black Sear ports of Varna and Galaz a plague epidemic has started. Young women in particular fall victim to it in large numbers. All the victims show the same peculiar wound marks on the neck whose origin is still an enigma to the Doctors<br>The Dardenelles have been closed to all ships suspected of carrying the epidemic. It is out of the question that the epidemic will reach Western Europe. |
| Medium close-up: | Knock's mocking, triumphant face assumes an expression of demonic grandeur. He straightens himself up, lifts up his head, raises his arms as if greeting the evil. |
| Scene 93 | **8 meters**    **North Sea** |
| **Title:** | **Open Sea** |
| Sea. | The Mediterranean. In the distance the "Demeter" sailing through the waters gleaming in the evening light. |
| Dissolve. Medium close-up | The ship's deck<br>The ship's mate is running up the companion-way in great agitation and crosses the deck on his way to the captain's cabin. |

| | |
|---|---|
| Scene 94<br>In the captain's cabin | **8 meters**<br>The captain of the 'Demeter' bent over maps, making entries in the log-book. The mater enters and reports excitedly: |
| Title: | Below deck a sailor has fallen ill.<br>He is talking in a fever.<br><br>The captan looks up, shocked. He leaves his work and follow the mate. |
| Scene 95<br>Below deck. | **12 meters**<br>In the background the ship's hold. Among other cargo in the deep darkness the coffins. To be seen through an open door. In the foreground the crew's cabin with hammocks In one of them the delirious sailor. |
| Medium Close-up: | Captain and mate go up to the patient who stares at them as if they were ghosts. He seems to listen intently. Every noise makes him start. |
| Shot of hold | Brooding, intense darkness. The lid of one of the coffins seems to open a little. |
| Medium close-up: | The captain, more angry than concerned, advises the patient in his uncouth sailor's way to have a strong drink. Promptly the mate produces his bottle and give it to the patient. The smell seems to wake him up from his lethargy and he takes a long sip. The captain tells him to have a good rest and goes out again with the mate.<br>The sailor alone. His eyes wandering . . .<br>Suddenly, they remain fixed, as if spellbound, on the door leading to the hold.<br>In horror he sits up and remains in a crouching position as if turned to stone. |
| Pan to the door leading into the hold. | There, horrible and awe-inspiring, stands NOSFERATU And . . . he . . . approaches. |
| Fade out | |
| Scene 96 | **10 meters**  Hornunger Moor    Lüneburger Heide |
| Wild and desolate scenery | In the distance a galloping horseman on the plain. He comes closer and closer . . . moving at tremendous speed. It is Hutter. |
| Dissolve<br>Medium close-up: | Hutter, standing near his horse and examining its injured hoof. With a desperate gesture, he lets go of it. Yet he has made his decision. He must go on. He takes the horse by the reins and walks on, dragging the limping animal after him. |

| | |
|---|---|
| Scene 97 | **12 meters** |
| Title: | The gulf of Biscay |
| On deck, the 'Demeter' | Evening. In the last light of the sun captain and mate are about to push the shrouded corpse of the last sailor over the railing. They have covered their mouths and noses with cloths for protection. |
| Shot of ship's side | The corpse is slid down into the water by ropes. |
| On deck. | For a moment the two last survivors pause in quiet contemplation of the horror of death. Suddenly, the mate's body stiffens, he has made a resolution. For a short moment, he shuts his eyes and tries to master the horror that is rising up inside him. Then he pulls himself together, tears the cloth off his face, takes up an axe and, brandishing it in the air, calls out: |
| Title: | I'm going down!!! If I haven't come back in ten minutes . . . |
| | With the courage of a desperate man he hurries over to the companion-way. |
| Scene 98 Below deck. | **12 meters** There are the black boxes. They are the man's target. He lifts his axe at the first one and shatters its lid. There it is: He is tempted to retreat. Rats! All round his ankles he feels the crawling of horrible creatures. Yet he pulls himself together for a second time. Another box, smashed by a second blow. And the same thing happens again: rats! only rats! He is wading through wriggling bodies which surround him from all sides. Yet he withstands the horror. There, a third box. |
| Close-up: | The mate. In despair, foaming at the lips, he prepares for the third blow. |
| Long shot: | The axe falls from his hand. His hair is standing on end. Quick as lightning NOSFERATU rears up from the box. Now the mate is finally overcome by horror . . . Covering his eyes with his hands he runs upstairs, crazy with fear. Slowly and steadily, NOSFERATU is approaching. |
| Scene 99 Fade-in. On deck | **8 meters** |
| | The captain is guarding the helm. Then from the hatch, the mate emerges . . . his hair has turned grey . . . his face looks crazed . . . he is foaming at the mouth . . trying to escape. . . he sways . . .turns deliriously in a circle . . .loses his sense of direction. . .does not see the railing. . . and overshoots it. Falling head first. The captain watches in horror. Now he is left all alone. But his face remains determined. He picks up a rope and ties himself to the helm, not to be tempted to leave. Thus he awaits the horror. . . |
| Fade out. | |

End of Act III

## Act IV

Scene 100  
Fade-in.  
A cliff by the coast

**5 meters   Heligoland**

Night, roaring surf.  
The storm is howling. A gigantic wave moves up, breaks the water splashes high up.  
**Moving coach**

Scene 101  
Anny's room.

**5 meters**  
Night. Anny is asleep.  
The storm is pushing against the windows, opening them. The curtain is billowing and fluttering in the wind. Anny wakes up. Confused, Terrified, she jumps up. She tries to shut the window, yet cannot bring herself to do it. The storm is pushing her back . . . she recoils. She runs out of the room.

**Waves**  
**Ellen**  
**Anny wakes up   Carriage**  
**Ellen walking forward**  
**Waves**  
**Carriage Hutter   Anny wakes up**  
**Waves**  
**Ellen Anny**  
**Boat**

Scene 102  
Ellen's room at the Hardings

**3 meters**

The storm is sweeping through the open window. The bed is empty . . . Anny enters. She knows at once what has happened, - rushes out.

Scene 103  
Roof of Harding's mansion

**4 meters**

Ellen, her clothes fluttering in the wind, her hair like a flag, is sleeping in the storm. She stretches out her arms defensively. A white figure against the black night sky.

Scene 104  
Scene 105  

Sea.

XXXXXXXXXX  
**6 meters   Contre jour   North Sea**  
High Sea.  
The storm is raging, enormous tidal waves . . .  
In the distance a sailing ship, the 'Demeter'  
at full sail, racing to its perdition.  
**Trick**

(Scenes 106 and 107 are missing)  
Scene 108  
View across the town at night

**6 meters**

The storm is tossing the trees.  
**Sailing boat moving towards it objective.**

Scene 109 is missing  
Scene 110  
Sea

**12 meters   Wismar**  
The storm rages violently. The sand bank threatens 'Demeter', the fatal ship, has closer, still moving at full speed.

View from the sea towards the harbor.
Sailing ships are coming in at full sail.
Contre jour (wismar). Trick
Ellen runs out from room
Broken axle
Ellen runs through garden
Ship moves towards objective
Knock 1
Ship coming into the harbor
Hutter running street. Knock
Ship in harbour. Nosferatu appears
Hutter running through street
Nosferatu through gate with coffin
Door Hutter
Knock escape
Nosferatu square or street
Room]

| | |
|---|---|
| Scene 111<br>Roof Balcony of<br>Harding's mansion | 4 meters<br><br>Ellen in Anny's arm. Her hair is fluttering in the wind. Ellen stretching her hands towards the sea, as if trying to defend herself. |
| Title: | I must go home. He is coming. |
| Scene 112<br>At the graveyard<br>View over the sea | In the foreground the crosses. In the back sandbank and cliffs. In the distance people, hurrying to rescue the ship-wrecked. The sand bank. The ship crashes into it . . . turns over on its side.<br>**View through archway: the sailing boat is moving past.      Weimar** |
| Scene 113<br>Lunatic's cell<br>Long shot: | 4 meters<br><br>Knock alone. He drags up a chair . . . to the window. He climbs up on it. |
| Medium close-up: | Knock pulls himself up by the bars, trying to look out. The wind, blowing in, makes his hair stand on end uncannily. |
| Scene 113a<br>The stranded ship | 10 meters<br>Dead and forsaken. a rope is dangling from the deck. It is swaying in the wind. |
| Medium close-up | An endless number of rats climbing down the swaying rope. |
| Shot of deck. | The hatch. It opens slowly. NOSFERATU climbs out. He carries the last coffin. Remains standing. Motionless. The image of death. Then he approaches slowly.<br><br>1) Ship anchored in the harbor. Dissolve<br>2) Ship's hatch with a piece of deck.<br>Trick:   1) Canvas glides away from hatch.<br>        2) Hatch lid is lifted.<br>        3) Rats are rushing on deck.<br>        4) Nosferatu coffin in arms climbs out. |

| | | |
|---|---|---|
| Scene 114 | | 8 meters   Lauenburg or Travemünde |

Scene 114

Town center.
Medium close-up:
    8 meters   Lauenburg or Travemünde

Trees, shaken by storm. A carriage races up, stops abruptly.
Hutter jumps from the carriage.
An axle is broken.
The coachman seems at a loss.
Hutter cannot wait. He leaves the carriage and runs off.

Scene 115
Archway with a view of the harbor:
    **5 meters**

**Nosferatu enters the town**

Scene 116
The roof of Harding's mansion.
    **6 meters**

Ellen's room at the Hardings'
Ellen and Anny. Ellen suddenly breaks away. Overjoyed as if she had a happy vision she throws her arms up and shouts:

Title:    I must go to him. He is coming!!

She moves off and vanishes.
Anny wrings her hands in despair.

Scene 117    **4 meters**
Storm-tossed trees. A white figure comes out of the house. It is Ellen. She is running through the park.

118    **perhaps Lüneberg Street**
Shuttered windows.    Nosferatu striding

118a    Hutter, running along the street.

Scene 119
Lunatic's cell
Long shot:
Medium close-up:
    **8 meters**

Knock, moving away from the window wall
The madman is listening for outside noises, as if he had received a signal from the other world . . . triumphantly . . . he whispers to himself:

Titles:    The master is near . . .the master is near . . .!

Long shot:    Suddenly, he listens attentively.
He creeps over to the door. There he waits expectantly . . .
The door opens. The attendant appears. He looks around the room. Not noticing that Knock is behind him. Knock creeps carefully behind his back. Suddenly frightened, the attendant turns around. Knock makes for his throat like a vampire. The attendant falls over. The madman is at his throat
**for a moment only, then he lets go and sneaks out.**

Scene 120
In front of Hutter's house
    **5 meters**
Hutter comes running up. He looks up: no light. He is just about to enter when - somebody is calling. He turns around Ellen!!!!! They fall into each other's arms.

Scene 121    Square with fountain    5 meters
Nosferatu, coffin under his arm, is standing in the middle of the square. Looking around to orientate himself. Then he strides on.

| | |
|---|---|
| Scene 122<br>Hutter's parlour | **4 meters  2x**<br>Ellen's sitting room<br>A lamp is shining. Hutter and Ellen. They are sitting on the chaise lounge. The happiness of being reunited was too much. Overpowered by emotion, he sinks down on her arm. |
| Scene 123<br>In front of Hutter's house | **4 meters**<br><br>**Nosferatu, staring up** |
| Scene 124<br>Fade-in. | **6 meters**<br>Hutter and Ellen, on the chaise lounge. He sits up, looking deep into her eyes. |
| Title: | Thank God . . . you are well . . .now everything has come all right.<br><br>She does not understand him. But the joy of being together again is stronger than anything else. And the room is bright. |
| [Scene 125]<br>Street in front of Hutter's House | **10 meters**<br><br>There is nobody about. But in the middle of the street stands NOSFERATU, hidden by the night, carrying the coffin. Slowly, he turns his head and looks over to Hutter's house. |
| Shot of Hutter's house<br>The deserted house | [There is a friendly light in the window]<br>**Empty! Carrying the coffin - Nosferatu appears in picture.** |
| Medium close-up: | NOSFERATU. Once more he turns his head. He looks over to the other side. The deserted house is over there. He makes for that now, walking slow.<br>**Then he goes into the house.** |
| Fade-out.<br>Scene 126<br>On the stranded ship | **12 meters**<br>The captain, collapsed in death, is tied to the helm. In the foreground, some men, Harding among them, are climbing up on deck. They are aghast at the terrible sight. |
| Close-up: | The dead captain. Tied to the helm in discharge of his duty! One hand is still on the helm. The other, holding a crucifix, clutches his chest in mortal agony.<br>His head sunk back, face distorted. There are two red marks on his neck . . . |
| Close-up: | Harding. He cannot comprehend the horror . . . |
| Scene 127<br>Sandbank harbor<br>Long shot:<br>Close-up:<br>Medium close-up: | **6 meters**<br>The stranded ship is in sight. It is night-time<br>In the blowing wind nocturnal figures . . .townspeople<br>Down the tilted hulk a man is climbing along a rope.<br>By the light of a torch! the captain of the harbor with a number of old people . . . Looking like fishermen. The climber approaches and reports. |
| Title: | Everything has been examined . .<br>No living soul on board. |

|  |  |
|---|---|
|  | The captain receives the report . . . jots down some notes. |
| Scene 128 | **10 meters** [Is inserted below] |
| On board ship. | Night |
| Long shot: | Back-board with helm. |
|  | Some men are lifting up the dead captain, and carrying off the corpse. |
| Captain's cabin: | Harding alone . . . he finds a book next to a masthead that is affixed to the helm. In the light of a dim lantern he reads: |
| Close-up: | A page of the book |
|  | Varna - July 12 |
|  | Crew - apart from myself the captain - one helmsman mate and five sailors. |
|  | Departing - for the Dardanelles. |
| Normal Shot: | Harding shakes his head. |
|  | He is puzzled. |
|  | **On deck. Harding emerges from the cabin with the book in his hand.** |
| Fade-out. |  |
| Scene 129 | **15 meters** |
| Fade-in: | **Daytime** |
| Port Authority building | A large hall. On the walls a number of figure heads Models of ships are suspended from the ceiling. The dead captain [is carried] in lying in state. |
| Medium Close-up: | Dr. Sievers is examining him. He notices the marks on his neck. |
|  | Dr. Sievers turns to Harding. He, too, cannot make sense of this case. Nevertheless he talks incessantly. Harding **comes closer** shows him the log-book. Both of them are reading: |
| Close-up: | The log-book. A page: |
|  | Second day: July 13 |
|  | A sailor has fallen ill with a fever. |
|  | Course: SSW. Direction of wind: |
|  | Third day: July 14 |
|  | Mate is talking strangely. He says there is an unknown passenger below deck. |
|  | Course SE. Direction of wind NE. |
|  | Volume of wind 3.6. |
| Normal shot: | Sievers and Harding are looking at each other. |
|  | Sievers' white beard is trembling. They continue reading. |
|  | Tenth day: July 22 |
|  | Rats in the ship's hold. |
|  | Danger of plague. |
| Normal shot: | Harding has been reading this aloud. |
|  | Now Sievers understands at last. He points to the book with his finger. Danger of plague! That's what it is. Danger of plague, he calls out. |

| | |
|---|---|
| Title: | Danger of plague!<br>Go home!<br>Shut all your windows and doors! |
| | Deeply frightened, the bystanders move away. The women put the ends of their head-scarves into their mouths. Panic-stricken .the crowd leaves the room. |
| Fade-out. | |
| | (Perhaps end of act) |
| Scene 130 | **15 meters** |
| Fade-in | |
| A deserted square: | Nobody is about. Except in the center of the square, the town-drummer with his large drum. |
| Medium close-up: | The drummer. He beats a mighty roll. |
| Medium close-up: | A closed window. The hatch opens and a woman's head appears: totally emaciated, sunken cheeks, long dishevelled hair. The disease has gripped her too. On her neck the ominous little marks. |
| Medium close-up: | The drummer has produced a piece of paper and reads it aloud: |
| Title: | All citizens are notified that the honorable magistrate of this town prohibits any movement of plague-suspects into hospitals to prevent the plague from spreading through the streets. |
| | The drummer has finished reading and goes off. |

End of Act IV

# Act V

Scene 131
Fade in.
A bend in a street

15 meters

A man emerges from a front door. He shuts the door behind him. Quickly and with circumspection he chalks a white cross on the door. Then goes on.

Panning shot:

The adjoining house. The man knocks hard on the door. From a window above a head looks out. There are still people living here. The man moves on.

Panning shot:

The first house in the side-street. A coffin is being carried out. Men carrying it have white bandages over their mouths. The man comes along and draws a cross on this house, too. Then he walks on, following his horrible business.

Scene 132

15 meters   2x   shaded candle on table near armchair.

Ellen's bedroom
Close-up:

Book-cover Inscription
(Vampire) See Chapter 1 of book.

Dissolve to:

Ellen by the window, the book on her knees continues reading, overcoming her aversion. Chapter II appears.

Medium close-up:

Ellen is pondering on what she has read. Hutter comes into the picture, with agitation almost hostility he grabs the book.
Ellen, standing now, looks straight into his eyes, turns and points over to the deserted house.
Compare the following
black dress and shawl
Hutter, black waist-coat and jacket.

Ellen's room.
Long shot:

Ellen by the window. Hutter approaches from the door

Medium close

Suddenly, she grabs his arm, stares out of the window pointing out, she shouts: There!!!
**Her body is tensed up like a bow trembling with excitement.**

Scene 133
The deserted house
Almost at once dissolve to window.
Medium close-up:

3 meters
Seen through Ellen's window frame.

A window, divided into four rectangular panes. Light from behind. Stuck to the window, almost completely covering it,
something looking like a black fourlegged spider. It takes a moment before one can make out Nosferatu's fingers which are clawing the window frame. In the center of the body, grinning lasciviously, the waxen face with ratlike teeth.

| | | |
|---|---|---|
| Scene 134<br>Ellen's bedroom. | | **8 meters 2x**<br>Ellen holds frantically on to Hutter's hand [shaken]<br>breathing heavily<br>She bends her head back. towards him saying. |
| Title: | | This is how I see it- every evening. . .!!! |
| | | She bends her head back. She knows all she has to know. And there is peace in the knowledge. Hutter has not come to that yet. He finds her calmness disturbing. He follows the retreating figure with his eyes. |
| Medium close-up:<br>Medium close-up:<br>Fade-out. | | Ellen is swaying.<br>Hutter, despairingly, presses his fist against his face. |
| Scene 135<br>In front of Hutter's house | | **6 meters**<br>It is now evening. The lamp-lighter comes down the darkening street and lights up the street-lamps. The he walks on.<br>**! remains!** |
| Scene 136<br>Fade-in:<br>Anny's bedroom<br>Long shot: | | **10 meters**<br><br>Anny crouching on a chaise lounge. Bent over her Harding who is holding her hands and trying to calm down the struggling woman who is shaking fitfully. She collapses with exhaustion. Then pulls himself together and decides: |
| Title: | | I will run over quickly . . .<br>I shall get Sievers.<br><br>And he is gone. |
| Medium close-up: | | Anny, having almost fainted with fear, comes to again. She opens her eyes. She lifts her head. Nobody around?? Is she all alone?? Isn't there something moving about in the corner? Something fluttering at the window? |
| Medium close-up: | | The window, covered by the curtain. Behind it the shadow of a giant bat.<br>It grows and grows. Soon it isn't a bat any longer. A vampire! NOSTERATU?! |
| Medium close-up: | | Anny's body hits the wall. She jumps up and pulls the bell. Then half crazed with fear, she runs into the background. |
| Scene 137<br>Anny's bedroom.<br>Long shot: | | Night. Servants running to and fro in the direction of the bedroom. |

| | |
|---|---|
| 137a | The bell is ringing. |
| 137b | Servant's room. A servant asleep doesn't hear, turns over in his sleep |

| | |
|---|---|
| 138<br>Anny's **Bedroom** | 3 meters<br>Anny pressed close to the wall. Servants are rushing in. There!<br>She shouts pointing to the window. Like a flock of chicken the women are huddling together. Anny rushes over to them, but they are already so gripped by fear that they imagine her fingers, which they are trying to push back, to be the vampire's claws. Shrieking, they run off in all directions. The door is slammed shut. Anny beats against **the door**. She is waiting for the horror, but she doesn't want to see it, much rather die first. She grabs a table cloth and covers her head and neck. Then she collapses. |
| Fade-out.<br>Scene 139 | 3 meters |
| Fade-in.<br>Ellen's bedroom | Daytime. Ellen by the window . . .looking out. She stands motionless. Paralysed by misery she witnesses the daily scene of wretchedness. |
| Scene 140 | 8 meters |
| Street in front of Hutter's's house | Ascending. In the distance, a strange procession is wandering across the street. One coffin after another carried by survivors. Past Hutter's house, towards the procession, a man is dragging himself along, tired to death. She supports himself by a stick. He catches sight of the distant procession and lifts up his hands to heaven in misery. |
| Scene 141 | with window -frame    Ellen |
| Ellen's room. | Ellen, on the point of fainting, turns away from the window She cannot bear the sight of this wretchedness any longer. She sinks into a chair, resting her head in her hands. |
| Close-up:<br>Close up: | The book, open. She has been reading it for days<br>A page of the book:<br><br>ONLY IF A CHASTE WOMAN<br>CAN FEARLESSLY MAKE<br>HIM<br>MISS THE FIRST CROWING<br>OF THE COCK WILL HE DISINTEGRATE<br>IN THE LIGHT OF<br>DAWN |
| Close-up:<br><br>Fade out. | Ellen lifts up her head, staring into space like a visionary. She knows. She shuts her eyes. |

| | |
|---|---|
| Scene 142<br>Fade-in.<br>In front of Harding's mansion..<br>Medium close-up: | 3 meters<br><br>The porch. Harding - haggard - a broken man, comes out. He closes the door and supports himself against the door-post. His hand reaches up, paints a black cross on the door . . .and falls down. His hollow eyes refrain from looking at his work . . . again . . . they cannot bear to see the symbol. He moves forward with a glazed look in his eyes. |
| Fade-out. | **Harding: black cape, dark trousers** |
| Scene 143<br>Fade-in.<br>In front of deserted house | 7 meters<br><br>Street<br>A group of emaciated men with a fanatical look about them are standing around. An unkept-looking woman is haranguing them. They are raising their fists. |
| Title: | He has been seen!<br>He ran out of the house!<br>He strangled the attendant! |
| Scene 144<br>Well in the market-place<br><br>Close-up: | 8 meters<br>Two ancient women are sitting by the well. Death has no terrors for them. Since every new day is a present to them.<br>The are whispering to each other; their heads are trembling. |
| Title: | In the deserted house. . .<br>that's where it is hiding.<br>He strangled him. The vampire. |
| Medium close-up: | Further back agitated people are running across the square, shouting excitedly to one another. The two woman turn around gesturing fiercely.<br><br>The clench their bony fists threateningly. Harding can be seen behind the well. He has heard everything. |
| Close up:<br>Long shot: | He utters a bitter and mocking laugh.<br>Harding walks on. |
| 144a<br>Street shot from above:<br><br>Close-up: | 10 meters<br>Crossing. Crowd gathering from all sides, then moving in one direction.<br>A street-corner with a man who points at something above. People rush up to him; they all turn to face the same way, look up, make threatening gestures<br>Somebody throws stones. |

Scene 145
Gable of a house          A figure is crouching on a roof-top

Scene 146 (?)
**Medium close-up:**     It is Knock. He is looking down with a
sneer on his face and pokes out his tongue
A stone whizzes part him. He suddenly gets
up and clambers off.

Scene 147                 8 meters
Ellen's bedroom           Ellen in an old armchair, busy embroidering a
cushion in the cross-stitch manner of the 1840s
An inscription reading:
      I LOVE YOU
She puts down her work, resting her head.
Tired, she falls to day-dreaming. **Then she lights
a lamp.**

Medium close-up:          Ellen takes up her work again, determined
to finish it.

Scene 148                 **Evening   4 meters**
Back of deserted house.   The street is empty. Knock jumps down a wall
and runs off. In the distance some men appear,
chasing him. They catch sight of him and rush
after him.

Scene 149                 8 meters
Meadows outside the town  Shot against a wide expanse of sky. In the distance
running figures, no more then silhouettes (Turn
slowly) Knock in front. His pursuers following
a long way behind.

Scene 150                 3 meters
Fields.                   Evening mists. Cornfields waving in the wind.
Suddenly, right in front between the ears of
corn head. Dishevelled hair. Then a bony back
The heads turn around slowly.
It is Knock.

Scene 151                 3 meters
A lane between fields.    The landscape has grown dim in the evening light.
The men chasing Knock are approaching. They stop.
They seem to have lost the trail.
Suddenly, one of them sees something. He opens
his eyes wide, shouting: there!!!
They all look one way. They dash off in that
direction.

Scene 152                 10 meters
Cornfield, Long-shot:     In the distance one can still the back and dishevelled head. Is it Knock? He seems not to hear
or see his pursuers. The men are coming near,
rushing towards him across the field.
They lift their sticks and fists.

Scene 152    continued
Medium close-up          A scare-crow. A black coat is dangling on a stick. Bits of straw and tattered rags. The men fall on it in the disappointment. Suddenly they stop. There! What can that be !!!

Long-shot:          A hundred feet away a head has appeared. Then the figure of a man. It is moving away quickly. The chase starts up again.

Fade-out.

Scene 153          **3 meters**

*Title:*          *Night*

Deserted house. Medium close-up:          Nosferatu at the window.

Dissolve

Scene 154
Ellen's bedroom
**Medium close-up:**          **8 meters    2x**

Ellen wakes up. She sits up in bed, listening as if she had heard somebody calling her. She gets up, walking as if pulled by invisible threads.

Long shot:          She goes over to the window. In the foreground Hutter asleep in an armchair, looking worn out.

**Medium close-up:**          Ellen is clinging to the window. She sees.

Scene 155.
Deserted house.          3 meters
Nosferatu at the window.
He raises his arms slowly.

156
Ellen's room
**Medium close-up:**          Ellen is about to collapse by the window. Shaking with fear she struggles violently with herself. The last battle.
Twice her hands comes up to open the window and drops down again weakly; then, with sudden determination, she pulls herself up dead straight and deliberately throws the window wide open.

157
Deserted house.
**Medium close-up:**          4 meters

Window
Nosferatu moves away from the window, turns around and disappears.

Scene 158
Ellen's room. Close-up:          4 meters
Ellen trembling with fear and apprehension

Scene 159
**Deserted house**
**Medium close-up**          Locked-up gates
Suddenly the gates swing open:
Nosferatu appears

| | | |
|---|---|---|
| Scene 160<br>Ellen's room.<br>Medium close-up: | 12 meters   2x<br><br>Ellen is covering her face with her hands, seized with mortal fear. | |

Long shot; window
moves out of picture

Ellen at window. She wants to call for help.
She staggers forward. She stops in front of Hutter.
One last moment of indecision.
Then she wakes him up. Hutter jumps to his feet.
He catches the trembling figure in his arms.
and carries her over to the sofa.
She begs him, hands raised as if in prayer:

Title:  Bulwer . . . Fetch Bulwer!

She entreats him to go. Hutter takes her hands, she
quickly kisses his head,
Then he rushes out.

Scene 161
In front of Hutter's
House.

3 meters

A path bordered by flowers.
Hutter rushes out.
Trousers, pleated shirt, collar without tie. No hat
no waist coat.

Scene 162
Ellen's room
Long shot.

5 meters

Ellen is still looking in the direction she saw Hutter
leave, then she gets up and walks toward the
window.

Scene 163
Deserted house.
Long Shot:

Nosferatu is walking forward and moves out of the
picture. The house looks more deserted than ever!

164
In front of Hutter's
house

Nobody is about. Nosferatu is approaching. He comes
to a halt. (He is preparing to jump, looks up)
He enters the house.

165
Ellen's room

Ellen turns around suddenly. She is shaking with
fear, anticipating the horror about to happen.
And it is coming - - slowly, tensed like a predatory
animal. She recoils, moves backwards step by step,
and step by step it follows her
      Heart! - Hand

| | |
|---|---|
| Scene 166<br>Bulwer's laboratory<br>(Living room) | 6 meters<br><br>In addition to the already familiar fish tanks there is a large telescope by a window. A profusion of antiquated scientific gadgets, globes etc. A lamp is burning. Bulwer asleep in dressing-gown and night-cap in the armchair. Cages with birds and all kinds of animals. Hutter rushes in. He wakes Bulwer, begs him to come with him. Bulwer starts to get dressed. |
| Scene 167<br>A municipal building on the period (town hall) | A large crowd is gathering in front of the town hall. Knock has been captured. More people keep pouring in from all sides.<br>Omitted |
| Scene 168<br>An office room inside the town hall | 5 meters<br><br>Sievers rushes in excitedly from the adjoining room accompanied by a man who has brought him the news. From the other side Knock is being brought in. The lunatic is trembling with fear.<br>exit |
| Scene 169<br>Ellen's room | 4 meters<br>Night. Ellen in bed, the strangler is at her throat, his fingers clawing her arms. Her eyes, widened in mortal fear, have a glazed look. Then she seems to have heard something. |
| Scene 170 | A cock jumps on to a still-life farm implements. He flaps his wings, puffs up his throat and heralds the morning. |
| Scene 171<br>Siever's lunatic's cell<br>Inside the town hall | 6 meters<br>Knock<br>Knock at the window, held by two men. Trying to ward them off, he shouts anxiously: |
| Title: | The master . . . the master . . .! |
| Scene 172<br>Ellen's room. | Nosferatu raises his head. He looks drunk with pleasure. Ellen eyes are full of terrible fear. She must not allow Nosferatu just to go. She pulls her arms around him: he cannot resist and bends his head over her again.<br>Omitted |
| Scene 173 | 3 meters<br>The sun is rising over the small town. |
| Scene 174<br>Ellen's room | Ellen's last moment of apprehension. There, isn't that a flicker of sunlight on the wall over her bed? Here eyes light up hopefully and remain fixed on this first sign of the new day. She stretches out her hand for it. And look: it is moving downwards. |

**Scene 175**
Street with front gardens

**5 meters**
The long shadows of sunrise. Nobody is about Then shoulders of Hutter and Bulwer appear. They are hurrying on and turning into a side street.

Scene 176
Ellen's room

**8 meters**
The bed is bathed in sunlight. Ellen's eyes are full of anticipation. Has she sacrificed herself in vain? Suddenly the horrible figure jerks himself up. He looks about in amazement. He clutches his heart. The bestial tenseness of his bearing relaxes. For a moment he stands, legs apart, as if trying to regain his balance. He clutches his heart again and falls on his knees, his face turned to the sun, distorted by pain.

Scene 177
**Siever's lunatic cell**
Town hall
Medium close-up:

Knock   5 meters

Knock, in a straitjacket, alone in the sunlight which is falling through a barred window. He is mumbling disconnected words:

Title:

The master . . .the master . . . is dead.

His head sinks on to his chest.

Scene 178
Ellen's room

**8 meters**
Nosferatu on his knees, supporting himself with one hand on the ground. He raises the other in the direction of the sun to shield himself from the light that brings him death. But he cannot hold out against the sun. His fingers, his hand, his arm are dissolving in the light. The sun seems about to strike his heart. Now his body is disintegrating in the light. Ellen throws up her hands triumphantly calling:

Title:

Hutter!

Scene 179
In front of Hutter's House

4 meters
Shot looking out from the doorway into the distance. Bulwer and Hutter are running, not just walking into the house.

Scene 180

8 meters
Ellen in bed. In anticipation, her hand reaches out for Hutter. Hutter comes rushing in, falls on his knees by the bed. He takes hold of her hand.

Close-up:

Her hand grasps his, the it lets go weakly and drops away.
Ellen's head falls over - - - -
Bulwer is standing at the window, hands behind his back looking out.

THE END

*Courtesy of Frankfurt Archives, Germany*

NOSFERATU
a symphony of horror
Based on the novel Dracula by Bram Stoker
Freely adapted by Henrik Galeen
Direction: F.W. Murnau
Costumes and sets by Albin Grau
Photography by F.A. Wagner
Music by Hans Erdmann
**Characters**

| | |
|---|---|
| Count Orlok | Max Schreck |
| Hutter | Gustav von Wangenheim |
| Ellen, his wife | Greta Schroeder |
| Harding, a shipbuilder | G.H. Schnell |
| Anny | Ruth Landshoff |
| Professor Sievers municipal doctor | Gustav Botz |
| Knock, a house agent | Alexander Branach |
| Professor Bulwer, a Paracelsian | John Gottowt |
| Captain | Mac Nemetz |
| 1st Sailor | Wolfgang Heinz |
| 2nd Sailor | Albert Venohr |

Authors Note: The best version of Nosferatu is available on Kino DVD

*Max Shreck*

Movie Magazine  September 1925

# My Own Story

### By Lon Chaney

In "The Phantom of the Opera"

"THERE IS NO LON CHANEY...
...I am the character I am creating. That is all."

*THIS has always been Chaney's reply to hundreds of questions asked about his personal life. No one has ever been able to learn anything of the man who exists behind the spectacular shadows we see on the screen.*

*In writing his autobiography, Lon Chaney breaks his mysterious silence of years*

**AS IS** quite generally known, I am not much in favor of personal publicity. I feel that an actor's private life is his own and should be disassociated, as much as possible, from his work. When I appear on the screen, I want the public to see the character I am endeavoring to portray— not the man Lon Chaney. I do not see how an audience can seriously consider an actor's work, if, through interviews and articles concerning him they know every detail of his private life—what he eats for breakfast, how many holes of golf he plays a day, and all that sort of thing. I try to dodge interviews, as a rule. Let my work speak for me. That's enough.

In relating this story of my life, I'm really breaking a rule that I set for myself when first I attained some prominence in the motion picture field. I shall talk of myself, freely, for the first time. I am doing this for just one reason. I have been told that the motion picture fans, who have made my success possible,

In "Shadows"

In "He Who Gets Slapped"

In "The Penalty"

In "The Tower of Lies"

**The parents of Lon Chaney were both deaf- mutes. But, as is frequently the case when deaf-mutes marry, their four children were all normal.**

**There were three children besides Lon; John, the oldest, and George and Caroline.**

Colorado, on April 1, 1883. I am of Irish and French-German decent.

My father and mother were both deaf-mutes, born without the faculty of speech or hearing. My mother's mother, Emma Kennedy, had two daughters and one son who were deaf-mutes, though she, herself, was perfectly normal. While they were still children, she became greatly interested in the problem of educating deaf-mutes and founded the Deaf and Blind State Institute of Colorado, at Colorado Springs. Her daughter's husband, my uncle Hugh Harbert, was editor of the paper they got out there for many years - the Colorado Deaf and Blind Index.

MY PARENTS had three children besides myself, John, who is older than I, and George and Caroline, younger. As is frequently the case when deaf-mutes marry, the children were all quite normal.

A great many people are inclined to pity deaf-mutes but I have found among them some of the happiest most contented people in the world. They are very social. Because the outside world of amusement does not distract them, they seek and find happiness in their own homes. Too many American homes of today have become merely a place in which to eat and sleep. Theatres, cafes, cabarets draw the young people and the older ones too—from the home fireside.

The "night life" with which the average person is familiar, is unknown to the deaf-mutes. They do enjoy going to the theatre occasionally, for they can usually follow a play by reading the lips of the actors, but the theatre is not as popular with them as it is with those who are not deprived of their hearing. Cafe life of course means nothing to them, though they do enjoy dancing in their own homes, and frequently give parties there. At their parties games of all sorts are played, and usually take up most of an evening. They get more real relaxation and amusement out of the simplest games than their more "fortunate" brothers do out of lavish cafe entertainment. And they truly appreciate their homes.

are really interested in knowing more about me personally. I feel that they have a right to some information, if they really do want it.

In the first place, before we go any farther, I want you to know that I'm grateful for the opportunities which have brought me such success as I have had. I never stop inside my own home, that I'm not grateful for it, for I've known so many years of wandering and of living, oh—just anywhere. I never sit down at my own table that I'm not grateful for whatever is set before me. I've known what it is to not have enough money for a meal—lots and lots of times.

I detest poverty, possibly because I've been so well acquainted with it. Money may not bring happiness— but the lack of it certainly does not. I don't ever want to be without enough of it to supply my material wants, again. That is one reason why my family and I live in a very quiet, unostentatious manner. We want to have enough in the bank so that if a rainy day does come along we can weather it.

But I suppose this isn't the way to start the story, so I'll go back to the beginning. I was born in Colorado Springs,

My childhood was, in most ways, the childhood of the average boy. I don't intend to go into detail concerning it, for I don't recall that there were any very interesting incidents connected with my early years. I went to school, played hookey occasionally indulged in the usual boisterous games of boyhood . . . grew older. I was always rather serious as a youngster, and I haven't changed much in that respect with the passing years.

**MY FATHER** operated a big barber-shop in Colorado Springs, and we were quite comfortably situated, until I was in my early 'teens. Then mother became an invalid through inflammatory rheumatism. Father spent a great deal of money trying to obtain a cure for her and , when his funds got pretty low he risked what he had left in an endeavor in increase his fortune. Unluckily for us, his business deals were a failure and we fell into rather straitened circumstances.

**I HAD** to leave school them, but even before that time I had experience in earning my own living. My older brother was stage manager of a vaudeville and later a legitimate theatre, and I started working props when I was still just a kid. My first job was at the Grand Opera House, and after one glimpse of life behind the scenes nothing could keep me away from the theatre. I was fascinated by everything concerning it. I used to stand in the wings and watch Richard Mansfield, Henry Miller, Nat Goodwin, Lew Dockstader and other popular actors of the day, and I absorbed a great deal of knowledge of stage technique from them.

I didn't care a great deal about school I was much more interested in leaning how to manufacture props—and at theater time a prop boy had to be proficient in the art of making all sorts of things out of papier-mache. I spent three years as an apprentice, learning this work and I'm quite proud of the fact that I'm a charter member of the Stage Hands' Union of Colorado Springs, Local 62.

I find, now that I endeavor to write of my experiences that it is going to be impossible to set everything down in chronological order. My life has been crowed, jammed. I've done all sorts of things, and during the early years I had a try at all sorts of jobs. There seems, as I look back now, to have been no definite pattern to those years. Through the theater interested me above all else, I did not spend my entire youth in it.

For a while I was call boy in a mining stock exchange. One year—the one following my fifteenth birthday, was spent doing housework. Yes, I mean it. That was the year when my mother became an invalid. We had a five room house and no one to do the work, so I took it over. I learned to cook , and very excellent meals I prepared, too. I was nurse for my mother, and I took care of my younger brother and sister who were still in school. I swept, dusted, cleaned the house as well as any housemaid could have done. These duties had to be performed, and it was up to me to do them.

For three summers while I was still in my 'teens, I was a guide up Pike's Peak. As you probably know, Colorado Springs is at the base of the mountain. My brother and I had thirty-three burros which we rented to ambitious tourists bent on climbing the peak. My brother took care of the burros, and I was guide. I used to take the tourists up to see the sunrise from the summit, 14,000 feet high. We would start at ten o'clock at night, have supper at the Half Way House, and arrive at the summit at three o'clock in the morning. I shall never forget those sunrises—the purple haze in the canyons—the clouds turning to scarlet and gold as the sun came up—the magnificent dawn blazing forth through the rainbow-hued mist. Though I witnessed it day after day, I never grew indifferent to it. Indeed though I was tired from the long climb, for I had to go ahead of the burros on foot, tramping every inch of the way. I would stand spellbound before Nature's supreme triumph, the birth of the new day. I would turn regretfully toward the prosaic downward trail when the exaltation of the dawn hour had passed.

The tourists season only lasted for three months of each year, from June until September. When it was over we took up other work and it was during those same years that I learned the window-shade, drapery and carpet-laying business, a distinctly down-to earth occupation. I really don't know why I took this up, except that I was interested in anything connected with interior decorating, I have some slight talent at painting, and the blending of colors has always fascinated me. I have an instinct for this sort of thing and, if the theatre had not already cast its charm over me, I should probably have made interior decorating my life work.

Four years ago I went to the Antlers Hotel at Colorado Springs for a brief vacation. I had to smile sometimes to myself, recalling that while in my 'teens I had laid the carpets and hung the window shades and drapes in the very hotel. I had been quite ambitious, I remember to become a real decorator and with this in view I spent three years with Cortdez and Feldhaser, a large interior decorating firm in Denver.

*The theatre cast its charm over him and no other work ever really satisfied him. It was when he was about eighteen that he allied himself definately with the theatre, having a natural inclination toward comedy and eccentric dancing.*

But, as I have said, the theater had cast its charm over me and no other work really satisfied me. I would give my attention to a new occupation with a thoroughness which I suppose is one of my characteristics. I never attempted anything in the half-hearted manner. I would learn all I could about whatever work I took up, whether it was rustling props, guiding tourists or laying carpets, but back in my mind was the thought that some day I would become an actor and identify myself prominently with the theatre. My natural inclinations was toward comedy and eccentric dancing, I could always pick up any step, being what is called a "born dancer", I suppose.

I really allied myself definitely and for all time with the theater when I was about eighteen.

I was working at that time for Cortdez and Feldhauser. One day I got a letter from my older brother in Colorado Springs, telling me that the local stage hands were going to present, "Said Pasha" a comic opera, at a benefit performance for the Stage Hands' Union. He was to produce the piece, and he wanted me to join him and assist with the production. I immediately gave up my job and went back home.

"Said Pasha" was a great success, so much so indeed that our company became very ambitious and we decided to stage "The Mikado" as well. For this we engaged professional people for the principal rôles, while the chorus was made up of local talent.

"The Mikado" was a hit, also, so it was but natural that we should decide to try out our talents in a broader field. We selected "Fra Diavolo" as the vehicle to take on tour. Mabel Day was our prima donna, her husband Leslie Stowe was the character man, Charles N. Holmes was tenor. I played one of the principal comedy rôles and also had charge of transportation and wardrobe. For my varied services I received $12 a week.

I was perfectly happy. In fact we all were. Most of us were young and fired with the spirit of adventure. There were a lot of hard times ahead of us, for we were one of the real old barnstorming companies, but we didn't worry very much.

We toured the state, playing mostly one-night stands. Charles Holmes, our tenor, had at one time had a company of his own on the road but had lost everything in a theater fire. When he saw that our little company was managing to get along pretty well, he made a proposition to buy it outright. We consented to this, and so began a three year tour through the Middle West.

When I look back at those old days, I realize how valuable my experiences were to prove in later years. A company such as ours could not be made up of shirkers. We had to be ready to jump in and do anything at a moment's notice. We had to be able to put up with a lot of hardships, be willing to eat and sleep almost anywhere, ride in freight trains. It was not a pampered life, believe me.

After we had toured around a little while, Holmes decided to make ours a repertoire company, and the Gilbert and Sullivan operas were included in our list of plays. With them we toured Oklahoma, Indian Territory, Kansas, Missouri, Nebraska, North and South Dakota, Minnesota, Arkansas, Texas. We certainly saw a lot of the country.

A lot of amusing experiences took place, of course. You may not believe one that I'm going to tell you, but is the absolute truth. We were traveling through Indian Territory—had a passenger coach hitched on behind a long freight train, The freight cars were loaded with railroad ties and the train was progressing very slowly, the ties being dumped off along the track at regular intervals, as they were to be used in the building of a new road through the country.

We dragged along slowly for some time, and presently some of us got restless. We were going through wonderful quail-hunting country, and the baritone, the comedian and myself made up our minds to hop off and shoot a few birds. The other members of the company wished us luck and we jumped down from the coach and made our way back into the country. We bagged a lot of quail in a few hours and then back we went toward the railroad tracks. We expected the train would probably have reached a certain point by that time, but actually we had to sit down and wait for it to catch up with us. It certainly was funny. Talk about "the slow train through Arkansas"!

We took the quail back into the caboose and cooked them. We had a regular feast that night, to which the trainmen as well as everyone in the company were invited. All of our meals when we traveled on freight trains, had to be cooked by ourselves in the trainmen's caboose. Oh yes, it was a luxurious existence, all right.

We played what was known as the "kerosene circuit," which meant that the footlights, in the "opera houses" where we presented our productions, were coal-oil lamps. Tin reflectors threw the light up onto the stage. I'll relate an incident which will show you how broad-minded the audiences of those days were, and how seriously they took whatever entertainment came their ways.

In "Said Pasha" was what is known as a "dark change" which meant that the lights must go out during a love scene between two of the principals. The lover would enter, and while speaking his lines to the heroine he would calmly go down to the footlights and turn them down one by one. This, when finally accomplished, left the stage in almost total darkness.

But the plot required that the Pasha himself should discover his daughter, the heroine, in the arms of her sweetheart. Now of course he couldn't discover them in total darkness, so when he came on the stage he would first go down to the footlights, turn them up again, and then make the discovery. The audience would take all this quite gravely. I tremble to think what would happen to a barnstorming company such as ours out in the "sticks" today. Lavish motion picture productions have made our old audiences far more sophisticated than they used to be.

Another funny incident had to do with what we called "hard tickets". We used to guarantee the audience that if they didn't like our show they would get their money back. For this purpose we issued special guaranteed, or "hard" tickets. Of course nobody ever asked for their money back—they hadn't the nerve—but the guarantee used to draw them into the theater. It was a good business move on our side.

Holmes and I used to take tickets at the door, Neither the audience nor ourselves saw anything out of the way in having the company's principals acting as ticket choppers as well. One time we hit a town, where the owner of the theater was also owner of a big dairy. We asked him if he had "hard tickets" and he said yes. I noticed, as I collected at the door that night that the tickets were a different shape and size than those generally used. I took some of them back to my dressing-room, when I left the door, and under the light I discovered that they were milk tickets. Adults had entered on a quart tickets, children on pints!

We were lucky, whenever we found a theater that had dressing-rooms. This happened very rarely, For the most part, we had to put up a sheet, dividing the space back stage. On one side the women would dress while the men would use the other side. There would seldom be room for our trunks back stage, and so these would be heaped in the orchestra pit. Between acts we'd have to go out into the pit, open our trunks, select whatever costumes we were to wear in the next act and carry them back stage again.

The audiences would interestedly watch this part of the performance. It helped while away the intermission time.

As our entire company including principals and chorus, included only twenty-three people, we had to do a great deal of doubling. This made it necessary to learn quite a lot about make-up, a study which always interested me deeply. I always took my work very seriously, as I have said, and any opportunity at difficult characterization, especially one requiring an unusual make-up, was relished by me. I like to play old men parts. When we put on "The Chimes of Normandy" I was given the role of an old miser. I was only nineteen at the time, but how I studied to make my characterization of the aged man a faithful one! I experimented with all sorts of beards and wigs. I learned to walk as a bent, feeble old person would. tottering around the stage in that part, I was probably the happiest person in the company, though I did not realize at that time that extraordinary characterizations were one day to become my life work. I thought that comedy was really my forte.

Those checkered years were filled with sunshine and shadow. We all had optimistic temperaments—believe me the members of those old barnstorming companies had to be able to look on the bright side of things—but sometimes we had to fight pretty hard to keep up our courage.

I remember one Christmas when we were all put to the test. You know how it is at Christmas time. If there's ever a time when you thoughts turn toward home, it's then. You want to be with your loved ones. You want to give them gifts, some visible proof of your affections for them You want a home-cooked dinner, familiar faces around your table. Christmas is one season of the year over which we all grow sentimental.

Well, our little company was far from home, and we were terribly poor. There had been a money panic in the country that year, and scrip had been issued. Everyone felt the hard times and, as is usual at such a time, the bottom simply dropped out of the amusement world. The theater is always first to feel a financial depression.

The day before Christmas we got into some little town in Florida. God, but it was a desolate place. Sand everywhere and just a few weather beaten, sunbleached buildings.

But we had to have our Christmas. It is never a day to be ignored, but the people of the theatre. Wherever they are, whatever their circumstances they will observe it as best they can.

A couple of the boys and myself went out and chopped down a pine tree, for what is Christmas without a tree? This we took to the town hall in which we were playing. then, of course, we had to have something with which to decorate our tree. So we all dug down into our trunks and pulled out all the spangles and dangles we could find—anything that glittered and would make a brave show. our trimmings consisted mostly of the harem belts belonging to the costumes worn in "Said Pasha."

Then we contributed presents, to be hung on the tree and presented at our little Christmas gathering after the show. Presents? We didn't have any money to by them with and so we had to make them. some of the girls made rag dolls out of bits of old costumes. I've always been able to draw and paint a bit, so I sketched the different members of the company in character. A few of our little group weren't able to get together any presents at all, so for the rest of us made extra ones for them to give away so they wouldn't feel too badly. Honestly it was pitiful. I've never forgotten that Christmas.

Well, finally we weathered the hard times and got back toward home. The show closed in Chicago, and the next one I went with was "The Cowpuncher" I was second comedian in that and got $14 a week. I only recall one thing in particular in connection with that play, and that was an accident that happened to me one night.

The leading woman was ill and another girl had to take her place. In one scene there was some business of her holding the villain at bay with a gun while I rushed on the scene to her rescue. She was to hand me the gun after which I took charge of the villain.

Unluckily for me, the new girl didn't know much about guns. When I went to take it from her she accidently pressed the trigger.

*(Continued next month)*

**In Treasure Island**

**WHEN the gun** went off and the wad lodged in my hand, I knew I had the rest of the play to go through before I could attend to the wound. There were five acts and seven scenes and through them I suffered the worst torture imaginable. I have a bad scar on my hand now. as a momento of that certain performance.

After "The Cowpuncher" I went out with the Frank Wade Opera Company in "The Beggar Prince," a light opera in which a popular motion picture actress of today made her professional debut.

We were playing in Champaign, Illinois when the prima donna failed us... became either ill or temperamental, I've forgotten which. We were terribly up against it. We didn't know where to turn, for there really wasn't anyone in the company capable of taking her place. Yet the show simply had to go on. The theater manager finally solved the problem for us. He said that his wife's sister, who was visiting them, was capable of playing the role. He brought her over to the theater and introduced to us Miss Myrtle Stedman. Miss Stedman was one of the most beautiful girls I have ever seen in my life, and her voice was glorious. She had just four hours in which to rehearse, but she sang *Zerlina* that night. It was her first professional appearance. We all knew that success lay ahead of her.

Our tour with "The Beggar Prince" had not been particularly successful up to this time. In fact, the barnstorming companies of those days hardly expected to reap a fortune from their ventures. If we made enough in a town to cover expenses and get us to the next town we didn't feel that we had much to complain of.

The "hotels" in most of the towns were a joke. I never stayed at them. When we got into a town I would look up a first-class boarding place and I usually had the luck to find a place where the food was excellent. Other members of the company, without my initiative would invariably try the hotels no matter how dreadful they were nor how bad the food was. But not me. I'd turn up at the theatre for the evening performance and make everyone else jealous, telling them about the wonderful boarding-place I had found and the excellent dinner I had just eaten. After their own dinner of leathery steak and greasy potatoes, they would become positively green-eyed when they found that I had dined on roast chicken, creamed potatoes, beaten biscuits and home-made pie. They declared that I had developed a sixth sense in the matter of finding accommodations. But it was only because I knew what I wanted and went after it. I've always done that.

A lot of people believe, or say they believe in luck. Well, I don't. Of course one may get a good break once in a while, but you have to be ready to make the most of an opportunity when it does come along. Like when I was given the rôle of the cripple, in "The Miracle Man." A great many people had never heard of me until they saw that picture. I was "lucky" perhaps, to be given that part by George Loane Tucker. But I brought to it all the knowledge I had gained in twenty-five years of stage work. I had started in when I was just a kid, as I've told you in an earlier chapter. When I was working as a prop boy in the old Grand Opera House in Colorado Springs, I can honestly say that I made the most of every opportunity given me to watch the work of the great actors who came occasionally to our theatre. When the other kids were out playing marbles, I was standing in the wings watching Richard Mansfield or Henry Miller, absorbing all the knowledge I could of their technique. Luck does not make one an actor, any more than luck found me boarding-places in those old barnstorming days.

Well, "The Beggar Prince" closed presently, down in Columbus, South Carolina. While we were discussing ways and means of getting back home, William Cranston of Winnipeg, Canada, heard of us, and came on and picked the show up. We jumped to Halifax, Nova Scotia, and started westward across Canada.

The Canadians received us very well. We played to crowded houses wherever we went. And, as the tour was so successful we kept on going until we got clear out to Vancouver, B.C. We put on "The Royal Chef" on this tour, and were rehearsing "A Knight for a Day" for the return tour. Naturally, buoyed up by our success, we thought that the trip back would be as easy as the one going out.

But we were doomed to disappointment. It is fortunate that theatrical people are, as a rule, of optimistic temperament, for they can never know just what is ahead of them. A play which may not seem particularly good in rehearsal turns out to be a tremendous success, while one in which the producers have complete faith, not infrequently is a flop. " A Knight for a Day " certainly was a flop.

We lost money from the day we started back with this play. The enthusiastic audiences of our outward trip had apparently vanished into thin air. Since there was nothing to do but keep on going, we kept on, hoping all the time for a more favorable reception in the next town we played.

But finally, having spent every cent of the money we had made on the earlier tour, we had to close the show, stranded.

Being stranded, strangers in a strange place, is no joke. It was fortunate for us that we had happened to hit a town where the people were kindly disposed toward us. They soon knew of our quandary and when had made it known that we were going to put on benefit performances to secure enough money to get back to Chicago, they generously turned out to see our show. We put on the benefit for three nights, and thus got enough money together to get back home.

Home, did I say? Chicago, when one is penniless and out of work, can hardly be considered "home." I had married some time before and now had a baby son. I will not go into details concerning my domestic life. Everyone who knows me knows that it is my policy to keep my family affairs out of the newspapers and magazines. I feel that they are a part of my life which belongs only to me, so the story of my romance and marriage to a girl who was a membeer of one of our barnstorming companies has no place here. As it is, I am revealing far more of my private life than I ever have before, or will again, for that matter. The domestic angle will be revealed occasionally, as it is here.

I arrived in Chicago with my wife and baby. The outlook was bleak indeed, but I knew I must find food and shelter for them somewhere. After tramping the streets for hours I finally located a cheap room in a neighborhood which was anything but fashionable. My wife courageously put up with the discomforts. After all, we had our sturdy little son to work for, so it was up to us to make the best of things as they were.

Having solved the problem of a roof over our heads, the next question was where and how to get food.

An opening soon presented itself. The musical director of our company had got a job playing the piano in a saloon. In those days the saloons served free lunches to the men who patronized them. At one end of the bar there would be big trays of sandwiches. They were real sandwiches, too, not the thin dainty ones that are served in fashionable tea rooms. Those sandwiches would go quite a way towards keeping life in one who was starving.

So I went to the saloon where my friend was playing the piano, and slipped out a sandwhich every now and then for my wife and baby. You weren't supposed to take any of the sandwiches unless you had first spent money at the bar, and frequently I had to borrow a nickel from my friend for a glass of beer, so that I could get the sandwich afterward.

Oh, I haven't learned about life from story-books, believe me. I've seen it in the raw. I've mingled with the dregs of humanity, and I've done it not on slumming excursions but because I had to. I've been on a equal footing with the poor, shabby unfortunates that polite society knows nothing about.

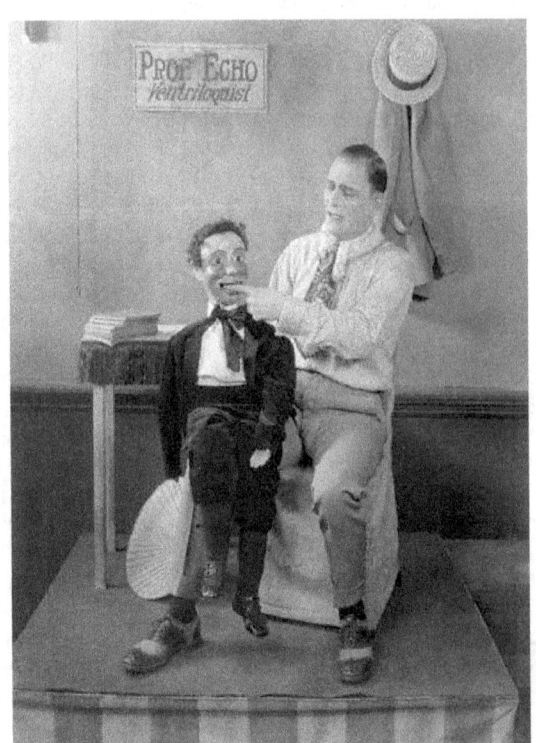

**In The Unholy Three**

*"I can remember going to the saloon where a friend of mine played the piano. I would borrow a nickel from him for a glass of beer so that I could get a sandwich from the free lunch counter. This I would take home to my wife and baby.*

I was always studying them, the harsh lines that life had left on their faces. If one had drawn a philosophy, or a hope from his experience, I'd remember that. I don't like to be reminded, either, of the old days when we all worked tobether down on Main Sreet. But we did work there nevertheless, and were darned glad to have a job of any kind.

Frances White was a member of that company. She has since become famous in musical comedy in New York, and is a headliner now when she goes out in vaudeville. But no one had heard of her then. Roscoe Arbuckle was our principal comedian. Bob Leonard, who later became a famous screen director, was also one of our crowd, while "others in the cast" were Winnie Baldwin, Arthur Hull and Carmen Phillips. We had quite a roster of famous-names-to-be, you see.

I was learning more about make-up and characterization all the time. With the number of shows we put on, and the variety of parts we had to play, it was up to us to keep abreast or drop out. We weren't pampered down in those Main Street theatres, let me tell you. I relished every opportunity to try out a new make-up, and, believe me, there were plenty of opportunities.

One Day I was sent for by a Mr. Dill, who later became well known, particularly in the West, as a member of the team Kolb and Dill. He was producing "The Rich Mr. Hoggenheimer and he wanted me to go with the show. This was something of a step up from the work I had been doing, and I accepted, even though it did mean going out on the road. My job was no sinecure, for I was stage manager and played five parts in the play, as well. I did a good deal of dancing in that show; particularly well.

It seems to me that I've given a pretty comprehensive account of those years and had passed since I definitely gave up all thought of other work and devoted my time entirely to the theatre. The early years, when the rosy promise of the future colored even our gloomiest hours, and the later years when, through struggle and discouragement I finally won some security and hope for the years ahead. This record is mostly one of hard, grinding work. But foundations if they are well built, require just that require just that, and I was constantly building a foundation for my future.

My experiences with Dill's show, and with others that followed it, are more or less a repetition of what has gone before.

But I was making a little more money now, though not much, and I was feeling increased confidence in myself as an actor. Although I had had a good deal of experience by now as a stage manager, acting was really my forte. My heart was in it, and I knew that it was really the work I was intended to do.

Being in Los Angeles, I occasionally heard something about motion pictures now. One or another of my friends would fill in at the studios between stage engagements. There were very few studios at that time, and they were mostly shacks with a fenced in space called "the lot." Costly locations trips such as the companies take now were unknown. The players worked out on the street or over in Westlake Park, and the pictures were all one-and two-reelers. It was only natural that in time I should become interested in this new brand of entertainment. But before I had a chance to investigate it, Kolb and Dill had joined forces and were putting on plays up in San Francisco. They sent me up there and, as before, I acted as stage manager and appeared in the shows as well.

I stayed with Kolb and Dill in San Francisco for two years. But before that time was up I knew that sooner or later I would venture into motion picture work. I used to drop into the little nickelodeons every now and then and watch the funny, jumpy films run off, and right from the first I believed that a new field of entertainment was being opened up to the public. I did not visualize the costly, elaborate film productions of today, none of us did at that time, but I felt that here was a new medium for expression, a new way of telling stories, a new theatrical enterprise with which I wished to be identified.

Lee Moran by this time had given up his stage work entirely, and was working for the Universal Film Company, which was then located down on Sunset and Gower Streets, in Hollywood. The Universal City of today, with its 480 acres given over to vast sets and stages had not been dreamed of. That first Universal Studio had once been a corral. There was one ramshackle building which served as a stage, and there were a few dressing rooms. Everyone turn his hand to whatever there was to be done, acting, set dressing, rustling props — everything.

At this studio I presented myself one morning, having quit Kolb and Dill up in San Francisco, determined to embark upon this new venture. Moran had told me the day before that men were needed out at the studio, and I was readily given a job —at three dollar a day. I had been earning considerable more than this with Kolb and Dill, but this new work compelled my interest. From the day I took that first three dollar a day job, I've stayed in motion picture work. The old days of road tours, of being stranded in strange places of seeking for a roof for my wife and boy were now behind me. My hardships were not over by any means. I was to know what it was to climb part way up the ladder, and drop down again. I was to know, even after I thought myself fairly well established in motion picture work, the experience of tramping from studio to studio seeking almost any sort of a job. Almost every sort of defeat and discouragement was to come my way, in my effort to establish myself on the screen. But I believed that in time some measure of success must come to me too. So I hung on, with perhaps a dogged determination. That's the only way you can get anywhere, I believe — by having faith in yourself, in the work you are doing and *hanging on*, no matter what you have to go through.

Louise Fazenda, Max Asher and Gale Henry were all in that first company which I worked. Jeanie McPherson, who is now scenario writer with Cecil B De Mille, had a company of her own. She worked as leading woman, and directed her pictures as well. After I had worked in a few of the Universal comedies, Miss McPherson gave me a part in one of her pictures. It was the first screen drama in which I ever appeared.

Jeanie McPherson seemed to like my work, and decided to write a story for me. Of course she soon discovered that I was greatly interested in playing parts that required unusual or even grotesque make-up, and she hit upon the idea of having me play the part of a hunchback in a picture. I often thought of that early picture, when I was engaged in filming the elaborate Universal production of "The Hunchback of Notre Dame," years later.

The hunchback picture which Miss McPherson directed went over very well. I should like to have continued on with her, but just at this time she left Universal and went to work for Cecil De Mille, who had recently formed the Lasky Company, working in a former carriage shop over on Vine and Selma Avenue. I stayed on with Universal and was placed in the stock company.

There followed years of doing just everything. I played in hundreds of character and comedy roles jumping from one thing to another with hardly breathing space. The two-reelers were ground out in one or two weeks' time, so there wasn't much opportunity for studying characterization. Nowadays I spend a great deal of time studying a character before I decide on the make-up I'll use in portraying it, and for some of my pictures I have spent three solid hours daily just getting into the make-up. But in the early days there was not time for elaborate preparations. At that, we made some pretty good pictures, and I did just as good work, in some of them, as I have ever done since.

I stayed with Universal for six years. During that time pictures increased in length from two to three, four, even five reels in length, and the day of the costly special productions was at hand. We moved from the modest little lot on Sunset out to the great Universal ranch. Player who had worked long, unknown, began to see their names flashed on the screen and to experience the first thrills of popularity and fame.

Warren Kerrigan became an idol of the film fans. He was Universal's most-popular star. The studio officials knew that I had considerable experience as a stage director and presently I was made an offer to direct Kerrigan.

I accepted the offer and directed Kerrigan for six months. But I wasn't given the chance to carry out my own ideas — do things my own way, and at the end of six months I went back to acting again. I like to direct, someday I hope to do it again, but conditions have to be favorable.

During those years at Universal I think I appeared in pretty near every picture they made. I was just rushed from one thing to another. Finally, it seemed to me that I ought to have a raise. I was getting one hundred dollars a week and I felt that I was worth more than that to them.

I went to William Sistrom, who was then the studio manager, and asked for a raise of twenty-five dollars a week, telling him I would sign a five-year contract at that figure. He couldn't see it at all, told me that I'd never be worth one hundred and twenty-five dollars a week to anybody. So after six years with this one studio, I quit. Once again things looked dark.

TO BE CONTINUED NEXT MONTH

*Movie Magazine* — *November 1925*

# My Own Story

by

*Lon Chaney*

IN THE long run, my quitting Universal proved to be a wise move, but at the time it seemed to be anything but that. For I was absolutely unknown off the Universal lot, and I couldn't get a job anywhere else. You see a character actor usually has pretty hard work establishing himself as a personality. With a leading man it is different. He is more or less himself of the screen, and if he does good work in a picture he is remembered. But the character actor must submerge his own personality in a role. There are character actors now in Hollywood, whom you have seen scores of times on the screen, men who have done very good work, too, but their names are unknown to you. Probably if you saw photographs of them as themselves you wouldn't recognize them at all.

A difficulty that the character actor faces, in becoming well known to the public, too, lies in the fact that his part is so frequently cut down to almost nothing in the cutting-room. The love-interest remains paramount, in the usual story, so most of the footage goes to the leading man and woman. Everyone else in the cast must remain more or less in the background. There are, fortunately for the character actor, some exceptions to this rule, and when a story comes along giving him a chance to really show what he can do, on the screen, he usually tries his best to take advantage of it. If he is equal to the part, he doesn't need to worry about the future, after that. *Tol'able David* established Ernest Torrence. Willard Louis, though he had been on the screen for a good many years, first attracted the interest of the public in *Beau Brummel*.

But the public had no interest in me, though I had appeared in hundreds of pictures during my six years with Universal. And the producers had no interest in me either., I went from one studio to another, trying to get work. I might as well have been an inexperienced extra man, for all the interest they took in me. At first I didn't take the rebuffs to seriously. I'd knocked about so much in my life that I could weather a few more discouragements.

But the weeks lengthened into months, and still I got nothing to do. It was not particularly cheering, either, to remember that Sistrom had said I'd never be worth more than I was getting when I quit Universal.

It was a good thing that I had always lived within my income, and had been able to save some money to tide over the months of idleness. But even with all my economy, my funds were just about exhausted when finally I got a job.

It was with Bill Hart in a picture called *Riddle Gwan*.

**LON CHANEY Says:**
"Many people throughout the country believe I am deformed. That is not so. I have designed a harness which I can wear for only ten minutes at a time. The pain soon becomes intolerable. But it is this harness which permits me to achieve the appearance of deformity."
Above: In Treasure Island

I want to say right here that I hope to keep Bill Hart's friendship for the rest of my life. He is a truly great man, and a gentleman in the real sense of the word. A lot of people don't understand him. He has the face of a sphinx, but the heart of a child. I was grateful to him, of course, for giving me a part, when I had been idle so long, but aside form any personal feeling I have always respected and admired him as a man.

Hart's business manager, who was with him when I went to see him, argued against giving me the role, He said I was too short to play a "heavy" with Hart. But Hart said that Al Jennings was a small man, but he had been a most convincing "heavy" in real life. He overrode all objections to me. Not only did he give me the part, which was a big one, but he left it in the finished picture. My work stood out, and the long period of inactivity was over. Producers and directors saw the picture, sent for me. I was at work again, and the really dark days of my career were over.

I did three or four more pictures, and then George Loane Tucker sent for me.

Now Tucker did not want me to play the part of the cripple in *The Miracle Man*. His idea was to get a contortionist who was also an actor. I am not a contortionist. I'm not even double jointed. It is just as hard for me to wrench myself out of joint as it would be for you to do it. It is only determination, a will to succeed, that gets me through some of the rôles I portray.

Tucker at first would not tell me the story, and it really seemed that we had reached an *impasse*, for I didn't want to go into something that I knew nothing about, and he, on his side, had great doubt of my ability to play the cripple. He had three or four contortionists under contract but none of them satisfied him as actors and so, finally, he consented to let me read the script and try the part out.

As soon as I read the script I was mad about the story. I'd do the thing if it killed me, and I started rehearsing the part —by myself of course. No one, not even Tucker himself, knew what I was going to do until the camera started grinding.

Since that unwinding scene of mine was the most difficult in the picture, it was to be taken first. If I failed in that, the part would be given to someone else. I guess I knew that my whole future depended on that one scene

**Bill Hart gave me one of my first big opportunities. But aside from the gratitude I feel towards him because of this, I respect and admire him as a man.**

**In The Miracle Man**

Tucker was standing behind the cameras. I knew by his expression that he didn't think I could do it. I read his skepticism in his eyes. And then he called *"Camera!"* and I flopped down, rolled my eyes up in my head like a blind man and started dragging my body along the ground. Tucker said just one work — *"God!"* — that was all, but I knew that the part would not be taken from me.

George Loane Tucker and I were the closest of friends from that time on, like brothers, really. He was another of the really fine men I have met in the motion picture profession. He death broke me all up, for I thought the world of him. A short time before he died he told me that he wanted me to direct one of his companies, and work in the pictures as well. But Fate had other plans for both of us.

Well, when *The Miracle Man* was released I received a great many offers. I was over-anxious to keep working, remembering those bleak months when it didn't seem that I should ever get another job, and I accepted about the first thing that came along., I played that rôle in *The Miracle Man* for one hundred and twenty-five dollars a week, and my salary remained around there for while, but I had at least proved that William Sistrom of Universal was wrong in saying that I'd never be worth more than one hundred dollars a week to any company!

My first lesson in being a good business man as well as an actor, came when I signed a contract to play the role of the legless man in *The Penalty,* for Goldwyn, some time later. I was the only logical person to portray that part and the company was willing to pay a high salary to secure my services, But I didn't know that —and felt that I was receiving a top-notch figure when I signed for five hundred dollars a week. Shortly after I had started to work, I happened to overhear a conversation between Mr. Lehr, one of the heads of the company and Clifford Robertson, the casting director.

"Do you mean to say," asked Lehr, "that you got Chaney to sign for five hundred dollars a week? I would have been ready to pay him eighteen hundred."

This was quite a shock to me. It gave me a knowledge of my real value to the company. But I can truthfully say that I've never abused that knowledge. I know that when a producer sends for me to do a picture he doesn't want anyone *but* me, but I've never held any of them up on that account. I believe in being fair, and most of them have been fair with me.

When I did *The Penalty* a great many people throughout the country go the idea that I really was legless. It would have been a relief to me, during the filming of that picture, if I had been, for I never suffered so much in my life. Every moment before the camera was one of excruciating agony, yet I must not let it show in my face. I had to be the character I was portraying, and disregard the pain caused by having my legs strapped back as they were.

I designed a harness, and had it made. I could wear it only ten minutes at a time, as the pain soon became intolerable, but, after a brief rest I'd put it on again and go on with the scene. That was work, let me tell you. I've never gotten over the strain that I was put too in this picture. In fact, every grotesque character I've played on the screen has taken its toll of me, physically.

The success of *The Penalty* proved that there was a place on the screen for the type of characterizations which I wish to portray. A demand had been created for them, and it has increased as time has gone on. My greatest problem, of course, is to find stories that are just suited to me. I have been terrible miscast sometimes and I know it.

Wallace Worsley directed *The Penalty* and then I did three more pictures with him, *The Night Rose*, *Ace of Hearts* and *A Blind Bargain*. I don't see any particular object in listing all the pictures I've appeared in. The next one to attract widespread interest was *The Hunchback of Notre Dame*, for Universal. I could not help but think, sometimes, when I went back to the Universal lot as the star of that production, of the six years of hard work I had

"The pain soon becomes intolerable. But it is this harness which permits me to achieve the appearance of deformity."

put in on that lot, and of the circumstances which had terminated my earlier contract with them. I had been told that I would never be worth more than one hundred dollars a week to anyone. *The Hunchback of Notre Dame* cost over a million dollars and it has paid for itself long before this.

It took a good deal of persuasion on my part to get Carl Laemmle, president of Universal, to consent to produce this picture. He could not see it as motion picture material. But for years I had a burning desire to bring the Victor Hugo classic to the screen, and finally I won him around to my way of thinking. It was not that I wanted personal glory out of it, but I felt that the picture would teach a great lesson. I hope that it has.

I wanted to remind people that the lowest types of humanity many have within them the capacity for supreme self sacrifice. The dwarfed, misshaped beggar of the streets may have the noblest ideals. I have come in actual contact with such people, the underdogs, the very dregs of humanity. Probably most of you who read this, haven't. When you see a deformed ,wretched creature you instinctively shrink from him. Your children are afraid of him. Older boys may mock and taunt him. But what do you know of him; really? Why he, like my Hunchback, may be willing to "lay down his life for a friend."

Again, as in *The Miracle Man* and *The Penalty*, I suffered constant agony while I was portraying that role. My body was strapped into a harness, which gave it the appearance of being stunted and deformed. I could work only a few hours a day, it hurt me so. I wore false teeth, which made it almost impossible for me to speak. Over one eye was a heavy lump of putty. When I removed the putty, after the day's work, my vision was distorted for several minutes. So much added strain was thrown upon my other eye, that I've worn glasses, off screen, ever since I made that picture.

But if *The Hunchback of Notre Dame* has given one person a feeling of brotherly love, of sympathy and understand for the downtrodden creatures of earth, I feel well repaid for all that I went through.

Most of my roles since *The Hunchback* such as *The Phantom of the Opera, He Who Gets Slapped, The Unholy Three*, etc., have carried the theme of self-sacrifice or renunciation. These are the stories which I wish to do. The picture which I have just completed, *The Tower of Lies,* is the story of a father's enduring love and sacrifice, even to death, for his way ward daughter. I do not know that it is my favorite of all the rôles I've portrayed, but certainly it is one of them, and I consider Victor Seastrom, who directed it, the greatest director in the motion picture profession. I have never been happier than I am at present, under my contract with Metro-*Goldwyn*-Mayer. Mr. Mayer, Mr. Thalberg, and other heads of the company, bless them, understand me, and are in complete sympathy with my desire to give the public real stories carrying vital messages to the hearts of the people. Frivolous, vapid stories have no place on my program.

I am finishing this story of my life, upon my return from a vacation up in the High Sierras. Under my present contract I am to have five weeks' vacation between pictures — the first real vacation I've had in twenty-five years.

Now, when I go on a vacation, I like to get just as far form civilization as I can, and my wife feels just thew way I do about it. I always take her with me. It's not my idea of a good time to go away and leave her alone. She's a wonderful companion, on a trip of the sort we've just taken. We rough it, live in a tent and she cooks our meals on a collapsible stove that we carry along in the car.

My son didn't go with us on this last trip, as he is finishing a business course in a commercial school in Los Angeles. He's going to be a business man, not an actor, though he has a strong inclination in that direction. A great many people of the stage and screen are willing that their children should following their footsteps, but I'm not, One actor in the Chaney family is enough.

It has been a long, hard trail, that which I have followed from the time I cast my lot with the theater. I've traveled the length of the land with barnstorming troupes. I've been stranded and hungry, and cold. I've fraternized with all sorts of people. I've tramped the streets of Hollywood, hunting for a job. I've learned of life at first hand.

But the harsh experiences I went through never made me bitter. Rather, they taught me, when finally things began to come my way, to be very thankful for everything good that has come to me, and for every lesson I've learned that has helped me.

I'm grateful for my home, and my family, and for such material comforts as I possess. I haven't any patience with people who become *blase* and indifferent as soon as success comes to them. I know I'll never be that way. Why just recently I got a great thrill out of buying a leather coat, before I went on a fishing trip. There had been other years when I wanted a leather coat, and couldn't afford one. I hadn't forgotten.

And I'm grateful to the motion picture fans who have encouraged me to go on, and to give the screen the characterizations I wished to present. If this story of my life has given you a clearer insight in to my reasons for portraying unusual, and at times grotesque roles, it has served some purpose, though I hesitated in giving it out for publication because I wish you to think of me as the character I'm portraying, and not as the man, Lon Chaney, when you see me on the screen. I have always wished to keep myself and my private life in the background.

There is one thing more. Thousands of motion picture fans write asking me for a photograph of myself. Please do not think I am indifferent to your letters, but, for the reason just mention, I do not send out photographs. I try to show my appreciation for your interest in me, through my screen characterizations, by making them as true as it is possible for me to do. I wish my work, alone, to speak for me in future as it it has in the past.

Lon Chaney, November 1925

London After Midnight, MGM 1927

The hat and teeth from London After Midnight plus the eye glasses from Mr. Wu - Ackerman Archives

Lon Chaney's first make up kit, formerly on loan to the Forrest J Ackerman Collection by the USC Collections

*Some of the roles that made Lon Chaney the number one Box-Office Attraction in the World*

 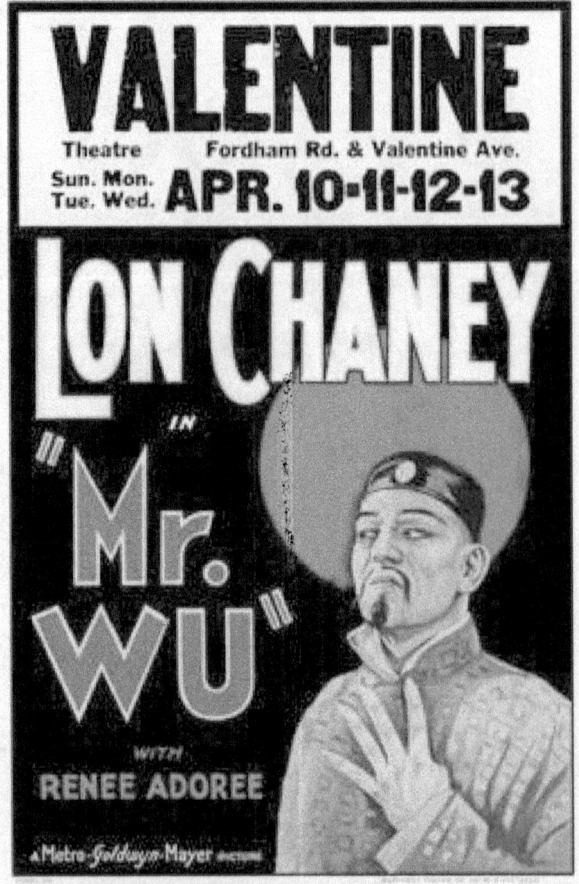